# AGATHOCLES

Borgo Press Books by VOLTAIRE

*Agathocles & The Duke of Alençon & The Two Wine Casks: Three Plays*
*The Baron of Otranto and Other Plays*
*Candide: A Play in Five Acts*
*The Death of Caesar: A Play in Three Acts*
*Irene & Tanis and Zélide: Two Plays*
*Oedipus: A Play in Five Acts*
*Olympias and The Temple of Glory: Two Plays*
*Saul and David: A Play in Five Acts*
*Socrates: A Play in Three Acts*
*Two Voltairean Plays: The Triumvirate and Comedy at Ferney*

# AGATHOCLES

## & THE DUKE OF ALENÇON & THE TWO WINE CASKS: THREE PLAYS

## VOLTAIRE

Translated and Adapted by Frank J. Morlock

THE BORGO PRESS
MMXIII

AGATHOCLES

Copyright © 2003, 2013 by Frank J. Morlock

FIRST EDITION

Published by Wildside Press LLC

www.wildsidebooks.com

# DEDICATION

For My Friend, David Ramsey

# CONTENTS

**AGATHOCLES** . . . . . . . . . . . . . . . . . . . . . 9
   CAST OF CHARACTERS . . . . . . . . . . . . . . . . 10
   ACT I . . . . . . . . . . . . . . . . . . . . . . . . . 11
   ACT II . . . . . . . . . . . . . . . . . . . . . . . . 28
   ACT III . . . . . . . . . . . . . . . . . . . . . . . . 47
   ACT IV . . . . . . . . . . . . . . . . . . . . . . . . 61
   ACT V . . . . . . . . . . . . . . . . . . . . . . . . . 73

**THE DUKE OF ALENÇON** . . . . . . . . . . . . . . 85
   CAST OF CHARACTERS . . . . . . . . . . . . . . . . 86
   ACT I . . . . . . . . . . . . . . . . . . . . . . . . . 87
   ACT II . . . . . . . . . . . . . . . . . . . . . . . . 99
   ACT III . . . . . . . . . . . . . . . . . . . . . . . 123

**THE TWO WINE CASKS** . . . . . . . . . . . . . . 145
   CAST OF CHARACTERS . . . . . . . . . . . . . . . 146
   ACT I . . . . . . . . . . . . . . . . . . . . . . . . 147
   ACT II . . . . . . . . . . . . . . . . . . . . . . . 165
   ACT III . . . . . . . . . . . . . . . . . . . . . . . 184

ABOUT THE TRANSLATOR. . . . . . . . . . . . . . . . 196

# AGATHOCLES

# CAST OF CHARACTERS

**AGATHOCLES**, tyrant of Syracuse

**POLYCRATES**, son of Agathocles

**ARGIDUS**, son of Agathocles

**YDASAN**, an old warrior in the service of Carthage

**AEGESTES**, an officer in the service of Syracuse

**YDACE**, daughter of Ydasan

**ELPENOR**, councilor to the King

**A PRIESTESS** of Ceres

Soldiers and Courtiers

# ACT I

*The action takes place in a square between the king's palace and the ruins of a temple.*

**AEGESTES**:

Heaven has finally taken pity on our misfortunes

Today it strengthens the bonds of old friendship.

When peace reunites Carthage and Syracuse,

Can you shed tears by the shores of the Arethusa?

Whatever may be our destinies, the places where one is born

Still have attractions for an unfortunate.

It's delightful to return to one's cherished country.

**YDASAN**:

It's no longer cherished and its glory is withered.

Its cowardly servitude and thirty years of misfortunes

Are souring my courage by tearing tears from me.

The volcanoes of Aetna, its ashes, its abysses,

Are less terrible than this region of crimes.

The sword that the Cyclops forged in their flanks

Was less harsh than the heart of tyrants.

Go, I hate Syracuse, Agathocles, and life.

**AEGESTES**:

What do you expect? For a long while, Sicily, enslaved

By fortunate Agathocles, has recognized his rule.

Agathocles is counted amongst the greatest of kings.

Chance, destiny, merit, perhaps,

Dispose of states, make one slave, the other master.

No man has ever succeeded to the rank of kings

Without sublime talent, without some virtue.

Let's be just, friend; I loved my republic,

But I knew how to bend myself to monarchic power.

Born a subject like us, hurled into the crowd,

Agathocles conquered harsh adversity.

Cleverness, courage, and especially fortune

Brought him to this rank whose dazzle importunes him.

Raised by degrees to the helm of state

He was already king while I was soldier.

With these blows of destiny I know they murmur;

The great success of others are an injury for us.

But let's not dissimulate; would we reject the prize

If it were offered to us?

**YDASAN**:

It would have been by me: I prefer, dear Aegestes,

I prefer my sad poverty to his funereal grandeur.

Excuse your master no further, and leave to my sorrow

The consolation of hating his happiness.

What then! I would have seen him, a citizen-mercenary,

The work of his hands nourishing its misery.

And civil war, in its horrors would have

Put this son of the earth at the height of grandeurs!

He reigns in Syracuse! And as for me, for my share,

Banished from my country, and soldier of Carthage,

Aged with dangers and bent under the harness,

Obscurely burdened with useless exploits,

I saw two sons perish in this iniquitous war

Which for a long while desolated Sicily and Africa.

After so many labors, after so many reversals,

My daughter remains to me; my daughter is in chains!

The unhappy Ydace is in the rank of captives

That the Arethusa again sees weeping by its shores!

That's what brings me to these funereal parts,

To the place of my birth a horror to my eyes.

Without support, without country, impoverished by war,

Deprived of my two sons, I have nothing on earth

But the debris of a fortune hardly put together

To deliver the child that the gods have left me.

I grasped the opportunity of the first days of peace.

I am returning to tear Ydace from slavery.

To the feet of your tyrant I am bearing her ransom

And, after avarice opens her prison,

I am returning to Carthage to end my career.

There, I will no longer see, hidden in the dust,

Mortals swallowed under the feet of a tyrant;

At least I will die free.— Go, serve in your country.

**AEGESTES**:

You won't leave without costing me some tears.

I bear arms under this king that you hate;

Our different duties have not broken the bonds

Of old friendship which unite the two of us.

I've seen your daughter Ydace; and sharing her pains,

As much as I've been able, I've assuaged them.

**YDASAN**:

You've softened me up, Aegestes. Is it near these walls

That she's dragging out her days and her obscure misfortune?

Where to find her? How to get near her?

**AEGESTES**:

Her cruel prison is in the ruin of a temple

Near this square, and not very far off

From the superb place where the king holds his court.

**YDASAN**:

A court! Prisons! What a fatal congruity!

Thus despotism is near slavery.

This palace is erected with marbles that once

Consecrated happy liberty to our laws.

Won't I be able to speak to my blood under these porticoes?

I've seen them decorated by our domestic gods;

But our gods are no more— Can I at least present

This feeble ransom that I am bringing?

Will your king Agathocles deign to hear me?

**AEGESTES**:

He no longer stoops to this unworthy detail;

His greatness abandons to one of his children

The profits of battle's debasing cares.

**YDASAN**:

To whom must I address myself in my sorrow?

**AEGESTES**:

To his son Polycrates, object of his tenderness,

And already, they tell us, named his successor,

All unworthy though he is of this excess of honor.

**YDASAN**:

I cannot see this king?

**AEGESTES**:

His somber distrust

Of all strangers forbids his presence;

With regret he permits his appearance to his own:

Thus it is that distance imposes respect.

Thus it is that, changed by age, and weary of the diadem,

He hides from the world and searches within himself.

For your daughter Ydace, a hurtful order

Will not prevent her from appearing before your eyes.

She lives separate from the rest of the captives,

At the temple of Ceres, secretly retired:

Her grace, her beauty, her charms more flattering

Than the splendor of gold or that of pomp

Cause hearts to fly to her feet as they pass,

Without her daring to think that they are rendering her homage—

I see her seeming to rest her eyes on us

Amidst the debris of the temple of our gods.

Weeping she is following this simple priestess

Who softens the sadness of her slavery.

**YDASAN**:

I endure the shock of seeing her,

Consolation is mixed with despair.

So then it's you, o my daughter! O unfortunate Ydace!

(Enter Ydace and Priestess.)

**YDACE**:

I bathe your knees in my tears as I embrace them.

I saw you, father, and flew to you.

Among the Syracusans, who has remembered you?

Could you have fallen into my funereal condition?

What have you come to seek here?

**YDASAN**:

The sole treasure that remains to me.

(to priestess) My blood, my dear daughter—o you, whose goodness

Extends a propitious hand toward calamity,

May the eternal justice of the just gods

Pay with a worthy reward the noble and tender zeal

Which gives to the great of the world, in these unfortunate times

Such a beautiful example, so seldom followed by them!

**PRIESTESS**:

I have weakly fulfilled the duty that engages me.

**YDASAN**:

I am coming to rescue my daughter and to take her to Carthage:

Protect us.

**YDACE**:

Alas! Your efforts are superfluous;

I am a slave.

**YDASAN**:

No, you won't be any longer;

I am coming to deliver you.

**YDACE**:

O best of fathers!

What! Your goodness will end my misery!

**YDASAN**:

Yes, I've collected the price of your liberty.

**YDACE**:

You, alas! The wretched debris of your wealth

Will not leave you more than a terrible indigence!

**YDASAN**:

Go, be free, it suffices, and my death is happy—

Have you, in your prison, appeared before the king?

**YDACE**:

No, how could he lower himself to me?

How could a conqueror, from the breast of victory,

From the height of a throne where his glory shines,

Be able to discern an ignored object,

Obscurely delivered from obscure misfortunes?

Does he know my fate, my name, the horror in which I am left?

By Ceres in these parts, this worthy priestess

Has deigned, in my captivity,

To cast on my disaster a kind regard;

Her cares have eased my cruel fortune;

I am learning at least to suffer by suffering in her company.

**YDASAN**:

I am going to find this king; I hope that his heart,

Although corrupted by thirty years of happiness,

Although hardened by time and supreme rank,

Will not dare to commit an injustice before me:

He will recollect that I was his equal.

**PRIESTESS**:

He's forgotten it too much.

**YDASAN**:

In his royal pomp,

Perhaps he'll blush at seeing my misery.

**PRIESTESS**:

I doubt it; but go, generous and tender father,

May simple virtue finally be able to touch him!

So that they let you approach his throne.

(Exit Ydasan and Aegestes.)

**YDACE**:

By our forgotten gods, beneficent priestess,

You are protecting me from the son of a tyrant

And from the misfortune that pursues me and favors him.

You who see the abyss in which my feet have plunged,

Don't abandon me.

**PRIESTESS**:

Alas! What can I do?

The ministers of gods whose sad character,

Once venerated, today scorned,

The still smoking temple, burned in war,

The altars of Ceres buried under ashes,

Can they, can my prayers, my screams, defend you?

**YDACE**:

Will they at least suffer that I return, far from these parts,

To Carthage where I was born?

**PRIESTESS**:

Agathocles has delivered to bloody and avaricious hands

The sustenance of his arbitrary laws.

Polycrates, his son, commands over the port.

The prisons, the ships, everything in this region of death.

All is his: the king gives him for his share

Sovereign taxes levied on slavery.

The captives are treated like vile bands

Destined for death, in circuses, at labors,

At the odious pleasures of a capricious master,

Prouder, more distracted than the king has been,

Polycrates counts you in the rank of those beauties

That he destines to serve his dolorous lusts.

Amorous without tenderness, disdainful of pleasing,

As ferocious in his desires as in his rages,

He's a young lion, who, always threatening,

Wants to ravish his conquest, and, roaring, love her.

No, no, his father was never more tyrannous

Than in naming this monstrous despot his heir.

**YDACE**:

Ah! How is it that the gods, always cruel to me,

Exposed me to his criminal eyes?

Between his brother and him, heavens! What a difference!

Argidus' humanity equals his valor.

This virtuous brother of a detested pirate

Has softened at least over my calamity.

Ought I to have some hope in Argidus?

**PRIESTESS**:

Argidus has virtues, and very little power.

Polycrates is master; he devours the fruit

Of the labors of an old geezer headed toward the sepulcher.

But shall I confess my secret alarms?

Argidus is a hero, your eyes have charms;

And despite the horrors of this frightful place,

Misfortune mollifies and disposes towards love

A prince born for pleasure, and who seeks to seduce,

Intends to establish his empire over our weakness.

Innocence succumbs to the tenderness of the great,

And tyrants are not the most dangerous.

**YDACE**:

Ah! What did you say to me? His generous kindness

Will be a new snare for this unfortunate girl!

I will have Argidus to fear in my fatal error,

And my gratitude will have deceived my heart!

In this distracted heart can you feel the wound?

In the heap of tortures that my youth endures

Is there a new one whose blows I must feel?

**PRIESTESS**:

Love is sometimes the cruelest of all.

**YDACE**:

Then what is my resource? Eh, why was I born?

Exposed to opprobrium, abandoned to chains,

The misfortune which pursues me surrounded my cradle;

Heaven returns to me a father on the edge of his tomb!

Far from Argidus, and from you, my timid youth,

There will only be another burden for his sad old age!

Hope deserts me! Death, only death,

Is it at least an end to the rigors of my fate?

Will I have enough strength, great enough courage,

To run to this port in the midst of the storm?

You read in my heart, you see my danger:

Ah! Rather deign to encourage me to die;

Firm up my uncertain, weakened soul

Against the feeling that ties me to life.

**PRIESTESS**:

Would that I, rather, by useful assistance,

Help you bear the burden of your life!

It weighs on all mortals, and God, who imposes it on us,

Intends, by having given it to us, to alone dispose of it.

He must have pity on your distracted soul.

Expect everything from a father and my friendship,

But especially of yourself and your courage.

I see it: you are struggling against a fatal storm.

God, my daughter, is pleased to see from the high heavens

These great battles in a sensitive and virtuous heart.

Beauty, candor, modest fortitude

Have often vanquished, the most funereal fate.

**YDACE**:

I throw myself into your arms: my desolated spirit

Believes, in listening to you, that the gods have spoken to me.

**CURTAIN**

# ACT II

*Agathocles passes across the back of the stage; he seems to speak to his two sons, Polycrates and Argidus; he is surrounded by courtiers and guards. Ydasan and Aegestes are near the temple.*

**YDASAN**:

There's that old tyrant, so great, so formidable,

That people think so fortunate! His age is overwhelming him,

His face, burdened with cares, seems to say to humans

That peace at heart is far from sovereign.

Is this he whose miserable infancy I saw

With our fellow citizens groveling in poverty?

Is this really Agathocles? How many brilliant slaves

Loan their servile hand to his shaking steps!

How he is surrounded! Their impenetrable troop

Seems to hide an unapproachable monster from the people.

Are those there his two sons of whom you've spoken to me?

**AEGESTES**:

Yes; you see Polycrates called to the empire.

He's said to be harsher and more inaccessible

Than this somber old geezer, once so terrible.

Argidus is more affable; he is great without pride,

And his noble virtue doesn't have a rough exterior.

Athens cultivated his morals and his genius.

Born of an illustrious tyrant, he hates tyranny.

The two of them are advancing towards the ruins of this temple.

Let's seize this moment, let's dare to approach them.

But especially remember, that Polycrates is master.

**YDASAN**:

Before him how hard it is to appear, dear friend!

**AEGESTES**:

In speaking to him, forget republican sentiments

**YDASAN**:

(striding towards Polycrates)

Prince, do you know the rights of mankind?

**POLYCRATES**:

Who's this stranger? Who's this bold one?

**YDASAN**:

A man, a citizen, an old soldier, a father.

**POLYCRATES**:

What do you demand from me?

**YDASAN**:

Justice, my blood.

I don't intend to tarnish the dazzle of your rank.

Why keep the treaties? Return young Ydace,

Sole escapee of the misfortunes of my race.

I am bringing the ransom.

**POLYCRATES**:

(to his attendants) Let them hide from my eyes

An indiscreet old geezer of injurious appearance.

**ARGIDUS**:

Brother, he's only making a fair request of you.

**POLYCRATES**:

Soldiers, obey when I command.

Let him be removed.

**YDASAN**:

Ah, great gods, return to me the time

When my hand served you and struck tyrants.

Must the sad decadence of my years

Leave me expiring at their knees without vengeance.

(Exit all but Polycrates and Argidus.)

**ARGIDUS**:

You could have responded to him with more bounty;

An old soldier ought to be respected, brother.

**POLYCRATES**:

No, brother; know that I will lose my life

Before my captive is ravished from my hands.

Neither the severity of my father's wrath,

Nor all these idle treaties that speak against us,

Nor the lightning of the gods aflame on my head,

Will take from me the object whose conquest I made.

My slave is my property, nothing can deprive me of it;

I am going to take her away from these parts instantly.

(after having looked at him for some time in silence)

Do you condemn this plan that my heart has confided to you?

**ARGIDUS**:

Who? Me? Do you expect for me to justify you?

What need would you have of my consent?

How could I approve such a distracted action?

Peace has already been declared with Carthage.

Agathocles swore it today on the altars.

All our fellow citizens have been returned.

If this Carthaginian has only a refusal from you,

You are reigniting the war.

**POLYCRATES**:

And that's what I am aspiring to do.

War is necessary to this nascent empire.

Where would we be without it?

**ARGIDUS:**

In these times full of horrors,

War has put my father in grandeurs.

To long sustain this fragile edifice

Laws are necessary, brother, there must be justice.

**POLYCRATES:**

Laws! That's an idle name of which I am unworthy!

Is it by the support of laws that Agathocles reigns?

He knew only two: strength and trickery.

The law of Syracuse is that I am to be obeyed.

Agathocles was master, and I intend to equal him.

**ARGIDUS:**

The example is dangerous: it can make you tremble.

See Croesus in Persia and Dionysius in Corinth.

**POLYCRATES:**

(after having looked at him again fixedly)

Are you trying to alarm me, to inspire me with fear?

Do you pretend to instruct Agathocles and his son?

I wanted a service and not advice;

I was counting on you—

**ARGIDUS**:

I will be your brother,

Your true friend, ardent to humor you,

When you demand of my fidelity, of my heart,

All that a warrior can, in honor, permit.

**POLYCRATES**:

Well! Serve me then.

**ARGIDUS**:

What plan is animating you?

Do you want me to serve you by hiding a crime?

**POLYCRATES**:

A crime, you say?

**ARGIDUS**:

I cannot otherwise

Describe the atrocity of this enslavement.

**POLYCRATES**:

A crime! You dare—

**ARGIDUS**:

Yes, I dare to teach you

The harsh truth that you fear to hear.

And who besides me can say it plainly?

**POLYCRATES**:

Go, that's where my unfortunate love awaits you.

Traitor! You haven't known how to hide my injury from me.

I see the imposture of your false virtues.

I didn't intend to discover my heart to you.

I sounded the profound depths of yours.

I've seen the recesses; I've penetrated the mystery

With which you know how to fascinate the looks of the vulgar.

I saw in my brother a fatal enemy;

He wants to appear just; he's merely my rival.

You are: you think to hide behind a mask of prudence

With slavery and with your unworthy intelligence.

More guilty than me, you dare to condemn me.

But you know your brother; he knows little to pardon.

**ARGIDUS**:

I believe you; I know your fierce insolence;

You think to exercise the power of the king, my father.

Mounted on the steps of this supreme rank

Are you alone here, born of his blood.

You are only the mud in which heaven gave it birth.

He knew how to cover it with the virtues of a master;

And your distractions have much disappointed him;

They've returned you to the rank which he left.

**POLYCRATES**:

They've left me this arm to punish a perfidious brother.

**ELPENOR**:

(coming to Polycrates) Lord, the king wants you.

**POLYCRATES**:

Yes, I obey—Argidus,

That's your last trick; but tremble on my return.

(Polycrates leaves.)

**ARGIDUS**:

I'll be waiting for you; we will see at the end of the day

If ferocity, threat, and outrage

Hide your weakness or demonstrate your courage.

**ELPENOR**:

What did I hear, Lord? What ardent wrath

Is arming before my astonished eyes your brother and you?

Alas! I've seen you enemies from infancy.

But what have I to expect from so much violence?

You make me shiver.

**ARGIDUS**:

Your advice is dear to me;

But I learned from you to brave the perverse.

I learned yet more in Sparta and Athens.

Elpenor, condemn my bold frankness.

I confess, my heart is no longer made for the court.

**ELPENOR:**

It is free, it is great; but lord, if love

Mixing its cruel weaknesses with your virtues

Ignites between the two of you these fatal quarrels!

They suspect it at least.

**ARGIDUS:**

Ah! Don't suspect it;

I don't know how to form an unworthy bond.

Polycrates, it's true, in his burning audacity

Thinks to submit to his rule the unfortunate Ydace,

And I cannot suffer this injurious right

That the fate of battles gives to the victorious.

I dare to brave my brother and serve innocence.

No, it's not love which will take up her defense;

I didn't know it; my heart until today

Had no need of her to avenge virtue.

Elpenor, believe me, if it's necessary that he must subdue me,

He won't drag out of me anything for which I must blush.

**ELPENOR:**

I have no trouble believing you, and my discreet looks

Respect the secrets of this generous heart.

But, lord, I would wish that a little complaisance

Were able to reassure the king of sad distrust.

He loves your brother; he fears you.

**ARGIDUS:**

Elpenor,

He ought to esteem me, and I dare say again

That the public voice, equitable and sincere

Would console me for the rebuffs of my father—

But what uproar, what tumult! And what do I see!

(A great uproar is heard on the stage: it opens, Ydace appears, followed by the priestess. The populace and the soldiers come forward from the back of the stage.)

**ARGIDUS:**

Is this Ydace? She—herself—in this terrible region!

Are you fleeing, unfortunate captive?

**YDACE:**

Infamously dragged by horrible soldiers,

Torn from the altars of my godly protectors,

From the hands of the priestess to whom, in my misfortunes,

Heaven had confided my fearful youth,

They pursued me still, distracted, fugitive.

When my father, overcome by the weight of my sorrows,

Went to the palace to let his tears speak

They seized his daughter in the name of your brother!

At this frightful moment their bloody troop

Recoils in surprise at your august appearance.

So much the just impress the perverse with respect!

From this respect, lord, I am carried away without doubt;

But the horror in which I am, the horror that I fear

Are my fatal excuse in this extremity.

And your great heart of noble humanity

Will deign in the end, propitious to my misery,

To save my freedom from the distractions of your brother.

**ARGIDUS:**

Yes, yes, I will defend you from this furious man.

This very sacred trust that I am receiving from the gods.

I am taking you under my protection at the peril of my life.

**YDACE:**

Through your rare virtues I am more enslaved

Than by this slavery to which fate has reduced me.

I detest life and I invoke death;

I live by you—

**ARGIDUS:**

Go: delivered from a tyrant

Revisit far from us your happy country.

It's all over, beautiful Ydace— Carry our regrets

For her departure; friends, let preparations be hastened.

(to the populace at the back)

Noble Syracusans, help innocence,

Embrace her defense against ravishers.

(to the priestess)

Priestess of Ceres, join with me;

Speak in the name of the gods, and especially of the law;

Let Ydace be free at last, and let them lead her to Carthage

With her worthy father from this shore.

(to the people)

Let none of you exact and let no one accept

The ransom this old geezer wished to purchase her with.

Freedom! Freedom! You were always sacred:

Freedom is dishonored when one puts a price on it.

(to the priestess)

Protect this object that I've returned to you.

Hide her virtue from persecutions.

Let her leave this terrible land today.

Ydace! Live long and happily far from me.

Go: flee especially far from a persecutor.

In making her leave, I am tearing my heart out.

(to Elpenor)

Will you reproach me that love may be my master?

Favorite of Agathocles! Learn to know me.

I honor virtue, misfortune softened me.

It's up to you to judge if love is swallowing me.

(Exit Argidus and Elpenor.)

**YDACE**:

Great gods! Who by means of

Argidus' hands are breaking my funereal yoke,

In your Olympus is there a soul more celestial?

Isn't it thus, that formerly mortals

By approaching you deserved altars?

(to the priestess)

Alas! You make my offended soul fear

That its pure virtue was not unselfish!

**PRIESTESS**:

I admire him with you; today I think to see

The blood of our tyrants purified by him.

**YDACE**:

They say that he was nourished in Sparta and in Athens.

He has their courage and humane virtues.

What modest grandeur in offering his help!

How my heart, which escapes me, is full of his speech!

How in defending me he was forgetting himself!

At the court of tyrants is it thus that one is loved?

I have nothing to blush for from his generous efforts.

They are not the effect of an amorous distraction.

His feelings are pure, and I am without alarms.

Yes, my happiness begins.

**PRIESTESS**:

And you are shedding tears!

**YDACE**:

I am weeping, I owe it to him; the excess of his bounties

His glory, his virtue—all softened me.

**PRIESTESS**:

Leave.

**YDACE**:

It's all over; let's return to the place that saw my birth.

Must I leave you! Ah! Why isn't he my master?

**PRIESTESS**:

Trust me, dear Ydace; from this day you must

Flee these dangerous shores menaced by love.

Your tender heart wants in vain to constrain itself.

Argidus and his virtues are too much to be feared by you.

Let's prepare everything, let's fear that his odious brother

Not bring crime into these funereal parts.

**YDACE**:

God, if you are protecting this weak and timid heart,

Gods! Don't permit it to dare to love Argidus!

Suffocate in my breast these secret feelings

Which will deliver my life to eternal regrets.

And by which, despite myself, the involuntary charm

Increases further my shame and my misery!

**PRIESTESS**:

O pure and sensitive heart, born in misfortunes!

Go, fear even virtue, and flee far from grandeurs.

**CURTAIN**

# ACT III

**YDASAN:**

I appeared before him, I saw him again, this king,

This hero once more unknown.

My deep sorrows subduing violence

I was able to control my revulsion and pray to him.

My features disfigured by the outrage of time

This scarred face covered with white hair

Didn't prevent him from recognizing

A fellow citizen whose eyes had seen his birth.

I astonished myself that he saw my tears shed

Without noticing the disdain that grandeur inspired,

Time, whose injury he begins to feel,

Could it have softened this proud and harsh soul?

With a softened look this prince commanded

That I be returned my blood as I requested.

Polycrates, indignant at the order of his father

Was unable to restrain his rage before him.

The barbarian left with fury in his eyes.

**PRIESTESS**:

Everything is to be feared of that audacious one.

His father has for him alone a blind tenderness.

One sees so much weakness with astonishment.

This king, so bold, so suspicious of all

So secret in his plans, so jealous of his power

Is softly submissive, like a vulgar man

To the proud ascendancy of a bold youth.

He doesn't love Argidus; he seems to distrust

This male virtue which he cannot imitate.

He outrages and insults this noble character.

He loves Polycrates; he cherishes his portrait.

The barbarian abuses it; there are no felonies

That his distractions have not soiled the palace with.

The father was a tyrant; the son is more so:

Without Argidus' virtue, and without this proud courage,

Your unfortunate blood, blighted, dishonored,

Was going to be delivered to cowardly Polycrates.

**YDASAN**:

He would have committed this affront to her unfortunate father!

**PRIESTESS**:

He would have dared it; but Argidus is a tutelary god,

A god who descended amongst us today,

Coming to avenge virtue and console the earth.

You must honor him, you owe him life.

Take your daughter away. A barbarian, an impious one,

Is still capable of attempting the laws of nations.

His terrible character knows no respect.

Put deep seas between him and crime.

May a favorable god guide you on the waves.

Remember me under a happier sky.

**YDASAN**:

Your virtues, your kindnesses, have surpassed my wishes.

Doubtless I am separating from you with regret.

But I must leave this barbarous region.

I must die free, and I am running on this path.

(Enter Aegestes.)

**AEGESTES**:

We are all lost: friend, go no further.

Death is henceforth the sole recourse remaining to us.

Argidus, Polycrates, Ydace—

**YDASAN**:

Ah, dear Aegestes!

My daughter! Ydace! Speak and give me death.

**AEGESTES**:

We were escorting Ydace; she approached the port

She was waiting for you to leave Syracuse.

The people rushed to the shores of the Arethusa,

Weeping over her departure, admiring her beauty,

Loading heaven with vows for her prosperity.

Suddenly, Polycrates, separating from the crowd

Appeared like a lightning bolt which cleaves profound night.

He seized Ydace: and with a detested arm

Tore his prey from the shocked populace.

Argidus alone, Argidus undertook her defense.

His firmness opposed so much violence.

The infamous ravisher, poniard in hand

Suddenly threw himself on this young hero.

Argidus fought; but with what courage!

You'd have thought a god against a savage monster.

Polycrates, defeated, fell and died at his feet.

The shouts of the citizens almost reached the heavens

And instantly bore the news to his father.

In his triumph, forgetting his wrath,

The softened conqueror aided amidst groans

The proud enemy who died threatening.

**YDASAN:**

You haven't said anything to me which is not propitious to us.

We are completely avenged.

**PRIESTESS**:

Heaven has done justice.

It's one tyrant the less in our calamities.

**YDASAN**:

Let's leave these parts, let's move— What have I to fear?

**AEGESTES**:

(stopping him) Listen.

The king, who put so much hope in his son

Ran to the very place, shouting to us: "Vengeance!

My unnatural son has just murdered my son!"

His proud soldiers assembled at his screams;

The populace dispersed, and fled with a timid step.

Distracted Agathocles has had Argidus arrested;

Your daughter was seized, and in his frightful trouble

The despairing king has proscribed the two of you.

**YDASAN:**

My daughter, just your name tears my entrails!

I hoped to die on the field of battle

Are we going to expire under the sword of executioners?

An old soldier must die without complaint.

But you?

**AEGESTES:**

If he committed that horrible injustice,

Ydasan, I can only follow you to death.

Despotic power is master of our lives.

We are without support, without arms, without help—

But priestess, can't you, as if dreaming,

Make your holy character speak?

**PRIESTESS:**

The time is no more:

Once the gods'

Empire was respected; their voice heard.

Remorse stopped on the edge of the abyss

Eternal justice shocked crime—

Tyrants have raised themselves on our downbeaten gods,

Enriched themselves with our wealth, wallowed in our tears

Declared war on our ancient rights.

Pride and rapine are the gods of the earth.

**AEGESTES**:

Let's separate; they're coming. It's Agathocles in tears;

He's a father like you, and I fear his sorrow.

Vengeance follows it.

(Agathocles enters with his suite.)

**AGATHOCLES**:

Let them take from my sight

This wretched object who causes me indignation and is killing me.

Over her and over her father keep your eyes open.

Let them both be guarded, let them be loaded with fetters.

Lead before me this criminal Argidus.

**AN OFFICER**:

Your son?

**AGATHOCLES**:

Him! My son! No—why this parricide—

My son is dead.

(they bring in Argidus in chains, escorted; Aegestes distances himself with the guards)

(to Argidus)

Cruel one! He died through your blows,

And you still brave my tears and my wrath;

And this blinded populace, seduced by your audacity,

Applauds your crime and demands mercy for you.

**ARGIDUS**:

Lord, the people are just.

**AGATHOCLES**:

It's going to be seen today

Whether this wretched prince is more just than they are;

Traitor! I abandon you to the laws I have brought.

**ARGIDUS**:

If they were dictated by justice alone,

They will conclude that in this sad battle

I saved innocence, and perhaps the state.

The name of law is dear to me, and that name reassures me.

**AGATHOCLES**:

Thus you increase your crime and my injury!

You never loved me and think to disarm me?

**ARGIDUS**:

My ever submissive heart sought to love you:

It is pure; it has no reproach to make itself.

This heart rose in rebellion when I killed my brother.

I felt the power of nature in me.

But it had to be combated and I've done my duty.

I punished felonies and I avenged innocence;

She had only me, lord, for her defense.

The cruel one forced me to pierce his flank.

Follow your wrath, bathe in my blood.

If, in this frightful day, remorse can be born,

I ought not to feel it—you may have it, perhaps.

**AGATHOCLES**:

What! Your fierce pride still dares to insult me!

**ARGIDUS**:

I only know how to pity you and to respect you.

**AGATHOCLES**:

(groaning) You tore my son from me!

**ARGIDUS**:

I defended my life

And I served you, I tell you, and my country.

**AGATHOCLES**:

Flee from my eyes, barbarian; await your just end.

**ARGIDUS**:

You are sovereign; command. I am ready.

(They lead him away.)

**AGATHOCLES**:

What am I going to become? Into what trouble he hurls me.

What then! His firmness, tranquil and satisfied

With an indifferent eye, an unnatural arm,

Come to turn the dagger in my shredded heart!

Now there are the worthy fruits of false wisdom

That Syracusans were seeking in Greece!

They've brought scorn on my laws,

Death even, and the hate of kingship.

So I no longer have any children! My old age overwhelmed

Is going to descend into the tomb without being consoled.

My glory, this phantom useless to happiness,

Illustrates my disgrace, by augmenting my horror.

What good's this glory and supreme grandeur do me?

I am deprived of everything and reduced to myself.

In the wretched days that may remain to me

I read a future which ought to shock me.

It's up to me to die: but at least I flatter myself

That all the assassins of my son Polycrates

Will submit with me to the most just death.

(to a guard)

You, watch over Argidus and walk at his heels.

(to another)

You, answer for Ydace and especially her father.

(to another)

Let Elpenor be found, a salutary advisor.

From his experience there is always a lucky fruition.

His eyes will clarify things for me in this frightful night.

(to an officer)

Sustain me; my soul, in its funereal transports

Has consumed the rest of its exhausted strength.

I no longer know myself. God of kings and of gods!

God that Plato announced in the home of our great ancestors,

I invoke you in the end, be it reason, be it weakness.

If you reign over us, if your high wisdom

From the height of heaven takes care over the destiny of states,

If you have raised me up, don't abandon me.

I imitated you, at least, by founding an empire.

And in giving it laws; and my sorrow aspires

At the end of the career I've reached today,

Only to avenge my dear son, so as to fall with him.

**CURTAIN**

# ACT IV

*Guards in the rear.*

**YDACE**:

(not containing herself within the boundaries of a modest sorrow, she must appear in disorder, her hair wild, and break out into sobs)

No, I can no longer hide my fatal tenderness.

I love him, I confess it, and love makes us equal.

No, don't control further a heart made to suffer.

I learned to live as a slave, and I will learn to die as one.

Don't hide anything from me; I can hear everything.

I know that in these parts the king ought to come.

He's an outraged father; he's an absolute master.

They say he's spoken; but what has he decided?

**PRIESTESS**:

He floated uncertainly; his soul demonstrated

Weakening sorrow and altered blood.

So much so that with a single word he froze us with horror,

And especially his silence inspired terror;

As soon as the depth of his somber thoughts

Revealed itself to the glances of a bustling crowd.

He sighs, he threatens, he calms down, he groans:

The only one they think can soften him is Elpenor.

His courtiers ranged around him fear him,

And in his despair he is the one who they pity.

**YDACE**:

They pity a tyrant! Low spirits! Vile flatterers!

They don't dare to pity Argidus! They close their hearts to him!

They think to make it a crime to take up his defense.

**PRIESTESS**:

The affliction of the master imposes a silence on all.

**YDACE**:

(uttering a cry and weeping)

Ah! Tell me, at least, answer my cries:

Is it true that Agathocles has condemned his son?

**PRIESTESS**:

The rumor is spreading.

**YDACE**:

I am dying.

**PRIESTESS**:

Dear Ydace!

Ah! Come to yourself! A father who threatens

Doesn't always strike. Daughter, reassure yourself,

Revive your wits distracted by trouble.

Remove from your soul such a dark image.

**YDACE**:

Argidus is condemned!

**PRIESTESS**:

No, I don't believe it.

**YDACE**:

I believe it too well— It's over with.

**PRIESTESS**:

It's here that the fate which awaits him must be revealed.

The fatal moment is approaching:

Agathocles is coming forward.

It appears that Elpenor is speaking to him confidently.

Let's wait a moment in these retired parts.

At all times they were made for sacred asylums.

Scorned by our great, the populace revere them.

I see your unfortunate father has already come there.

**YDACE**:

They will come to tear him from your holy asylum.

Who can hide from the glance of a tyrant?

(Agathocles enters on one side followed by Elpenor. Ydasan, Ydace, and the Priestess are withdrawn in the ruins of the temple on the other.)

**AGATHOCLES**:

(to Elpenor)

Yes, I tell you, the traitor irritates my wrath;

With his forced respect he insults his father.

Seeing Argidus near me, you would have said

That I was the guilty one, and that Argidus was king.

The insolent one boasted of his crime to my face.

The murder of his brother, is, he says, legitimate.

He served the state by tearing my son from me!

(he sits)

It's too much! Let them avenge me—Elpenor, obey.

Let them avenge me.— Soldiers, don't spare Argidus any longer.

A king must punish a parricide.

Let him die.

**PRIESTESS** (rushing from her asylum and throwing herself at Agathocles' knees.)

No, lord, no, you don't want

To contemplate the death of two sons in one day.

You will not sacrifice half of yourself.

The supreme majesty of my scorned gods

Is not speaking here with my feeble voice.

I will no longer attest their justice and their laws.

I know too well the slow action of their eternal vengeance

In pursuit of the criminal heads of evil kings;

And that often lightning bursts in idle bolts

For hardened hearts who do not fear it.

But don't ruin yourself on such a funereal day.

Don't avenge one son on the son that remains to you.

And don't deprive yourself of the only succor

That heaven keeps for you in your unfortunate life.

**YDASAN**:

Cruel man! Can you strike an innocent girl!

**YDACE**:

I bring my head here, and your bloody hand

Will favor me by making me die.

But see the horrors in which you are going to run.

The son whose very deserved death you are weeping for

Had an atrocious soul infected with crime

And jealous of his brother was going to murder him.

The son that an unjust father dares here to condemn

Is a hero, a god who did us justice.

If you determinately will his death,

See already this blood shed by your hands,

Gods and humans rise against you.

You will be detested by all of nature.

Detested for yourself—and the august and pure soul,

The soul of great Argidus, vainly from the height of the heavens

Will implore for you the clemency of the gods.

They will follow your example: they will be without mercy.

This very precious blood will shriek loudly for vengeance.

The truth is rising to your deceived eyes.

It led our voices—I await death; strike.

**AGATHOCLES**:

What! These three enemies are insulting my loss!

What! Under their trembling feet when the tomb is opened

They are still tearing up this desperate heart!

Make them leave!

(They are led away.)

My distracted wits

From all I am hearing receives frightful omens.

Friend, during thirty years of labors and storms

Tested each day by new perils,

Never has a day risen more frightful to me.

My son had his faults; paternal friendship

Doesn't paint an unfaithful image to me.

But his lofty courage seconded my plans,

He supported the throne established by my hands.

And, it's necessary to reveal my thoughts to your view.

My old age wearied of this bloody throne

Was going to resign it to my unfortunate son.

You see what effects my plans have followed.

My heart is opening to your eyes; open yours to mine.

Tell me the truth; I fear it but I love it.

Is it true that my sons were fighting, both of them,

Over this young beauty, this dangerous creature,

This slave?

**ELPENOR**:

It's pretended that they burned for her.

This love produced their bloody quarrel.

She caused the death of the son that you are weeping for.

Polycrates, scorning your sacred orders

By raising over Ydace a bold hand,

Raised the dagger against his unfortunate brother.

Argidus is courageous; he didn't belie

The pure blood of a hero from which he's seen to come.

I moan with you that this intrepid son

With so much virtue is only a parricide.

But Polycrates was the unjust aggressor.

**AGATHOCLES**:

The two of them are criminals; they've pierced my heart.

The one succumbed to death, and the other deserves it.

Against the murderer you know all that irritates me.

His popular favor must have alarmed me.

He offended me especially by making himself loved.

His name thrived in the ruins of my glory.

In vain in the West the hands of Victory

Have crowned me a hundred times with laurels.

In my sad house I was abandoned—

I am forever. I feel too keenly that the envy

Of the tortures that I am enduring is hardly glutted.

They hate me, and there's the envenomed feature

That pierces a withered heart consumed by boredom—

But Argidus is my son.

**ELPENOR**:

And I dare yet tell you

That he is worthy of being so, and worthy of the empire,

Incapable of feigning as of flattering,

Of suffering an affront and of deserving it.

Virtuous and sensitive—

**AGATHOCLES**:

Ah! What are you daring to contend?

Him, sensitive! Did he deign to give in to my tears?

Had he remorse for the murder of his brother?

Has he made some tentative efforts to soften me?

Eh! Didn't he brave the sorrow of his father?

**ELPENOR**:

There's too much pride in this great character:

He doesn't know how to bend,

**AGATHOCLES**:

I must know how to punish.

**ELPENOR**:

Don't prepare a horrible future.

Nature has spoken; its voice is always tender,

**AGATHOCLES**:

The shout of vengeance is also making itself heard.

I owe everything to my throne! O embloodied throne!

So brilliant, so funereal, and so dearly bought!

Dazzling grandeur, and what evil I have known!

To what degree will your shining seduce my gaze?

**ELPENOR**:

Of the trouble wherein I see you, what must this presage?

What do you decree for a son?

**AGATHOCLES**:

Let me breathe.

**CURTAIN**

# ACT V

*The Priestess and Ydasan by the temple at the front of the stage. Guards at the back.*

**PRIESTESS**:

Astonishing examples of the caprices of fate!

In this region of death, unknown to one another

Under the fetters of a tyrant, a prison joins us back together.

And I've seen you only to die together!

O unfortunate father! It's in these same parts

In this temple where formerly our gods descended,

It's in the debris of the ashes of their altars

That the king is going to appear, and the execution must take place!

Agathocles intends that his servile court

Solemnize with him this deplorable day.

It's an august ceremonial: and his afflicted soul

Thinks that by this great glitter his loss will be better avenged.

He thinks to instruct better a shocked populace

That the blood of a tyrant must be respected.

All must bend beneath his powerful voice—

And they call this horrible spectacle justice!

**YDASAN**:

Priestess, believe me, this violent wrath

Surfeited with blood won't reach you.

There are, there's no doubt of it, sacred barriers

Whose revered limits one doesn't cross.

A tyrant fears the people; and this people, in my eyes

All corrupted though it is, respects its gods in you.

After all, you are not the accomplice of my daughter.

It's enough that an unfortunate perish with her.

That's my sole prayer: and the blow that awaits me

Can advance my death by only a moment.

I am leaving you softened; pardon my tears.

**PRIESTESS**:

They're not permitted; these armed informers

Are going to our tyrant to report our conversation.

**YDASAN**:

I know it; it's the custom established in courts.

Great gods! I see Argidus appearing with Ydace!

**ARGIDUS:** (entering, guards at the back)

It's permitted; I am coming to seek mercy here.

**YDASAN**:

Lord, what are you saying?

**ARGIDUS**:

I defended your daughter

Against her ravisher, and avenged her honor.

I've done more; I loved her and sacrificing myself for her,

I imposed on myself an eternal absence.

I ask of you here, the reward of her virtue

For which I am going to die, for which I fought.

I stifled my love, and I was unable to pretend

—Misfortune of being a prince—to become your son-in-law.

But in the end, I am very honored by this name.

I want to bear that sacred name in my tomb.

Ydace, let my dying hand press yours,

Loving each other, we will expire for one another.

May my eyes be still fixed on your eyes,

May the divinity which nourished our ancestors

Preside with marriage at our fatal hour.

(to priestess)

O priestess, light the nuptial torch.

(to Ydasan)

Hug us, my father, in our last moments.

Ydace, dear Ydace, accept my oaths.

They are pure like you: our conjoined souls

Are being recalled to heaven which created them.

Protect, if possible, a just future,

The most holy eternal memory of love.

**YDACE**:

(to Ydasan) Argidus' feelings have entered my soul;

His courage raises me, and his virtue inflames me.

The name of his spouse is too fine a title

For you to refuse to decorate my tomb with it.

No, Argidus, with you death is not cruel;

Life is transient, and glory is immortal.

**YDASAN**:

Ah, my prince, my daughter!

**PRIESTESS**:

Unfortunate spouses!

Couple worthy of heaven! It is open for you;

It sees a great spectacle, and worthy of admiration,

Virtue combatting tyranny.

**YDASAN**:

Dear daughter! Great prince! In what a horrible day,

In what horrible places you speak to me of love!

Well, I unite you; well, gods that I affirm,

Gods of the unfortunates, form this funereal bond.

And to celebrate it, overthrow our tyrants

Into the abyss where lightning hurled the Titans!

Let the flame of Aetna illuminate these chasms!

Let the barbarian fall into it, live there, and be consumed by it!

Let his just death, forever repeated

Be the eternal vengeance of my innocent blood,

And Sicily and Syracuse fall into powder

If the oppressor of the people escapes the thunderbolt.

Those are my wishes for you, dear and tender lovers,

Both our wedding songs and my last oaths.

**PRIESTESS**:

Our time has come; Agathocles is coming forward:

He is adding to death the horror of his presence.

**ARGIDUS**:

What! His court surrounds him and the people are following him!

**YDASAN**:

What demon, what intrigue, is leading him to us?

(Enter Agathocles surrounded by his court. The populace arranges itself on both side of the stage, the great take their place around the throne and remain standing.)

**AGATHOCLES**:

Tempered Justice—its voice dictates the sentence—

(he mounts his throne that has been brought in and sits on it)

It's I who am announcing it to you: listen in silence—

You see me on the throne, it's the worthy reward

For thirty years of labor undertaken for the State.

I was ambitious, I make no excuse for it;

And if with some glory, on the plains of Syracuse

Amongst so many battles, I was able to cover my name,

That glory was the fruit of my ambition.

If it was a fault, it was a heroic fault.

I was born unknown in your republic.

I was base, and I owe everything to myself,

The talents, the virtues which made me your king.

I didn't need an illustrious origin.

Mine added a new luster to my grandeur

Potter's clay once molded by my hands

Produced the gold which crowned my face.

Seized with glory and with so much power

Still, I felt a sad insufficiency.

—I see plainly, heaven places in the depths of our hearts

A secret feeling above grandeurs;

I experienced it and my soul is much stronger still

To disdain the dazzle adored by the vulgar.

Having consulted myself carefully, I can equally

Live and die on the throne or in obscurity.

—For a son that I loved, my prodigal tenderness

Made me hope that in the days of my old age

He would sustain the weight of my powerful empire.

I thought him worthy of ruling you.

I was abused; these deceitful errors

Are the common share of kings and fathers.

It's little to know them, they must be expiated.

O my son, in my arms, deign to forget them.

(he takes Argidus in his arms and makes him sit beside him)

People, here's the king you must recognize.

I trust all is repaired, I am making him your master.

Yes, my son, I knew that in this sad day

Virtue would win out over the most tender love.

You deserve Ydace as well as my crown.

Enjoy them both; your father gives them to you.

Priestess of Ceres, light the torches

Which must lighten such beautiful triumphs.

Rebuild your altars, celebrate your mysteries

That I thought too great for my contrary power.

Teach the people to fulfill, at the same time,

What is owed to gods and what is owed to kings

—You generous warrior, you, father of Ydace!

May you see your blood reborn in my race!

Serve as father to my son, give me your friendship.

Pardon the sovereign who forgot you,

Pardon these grandeurs that heaven is delivering me from.

The prince has vanished; the man begins to live.

**YDACE**:

(to the priestess) O gods!

**AEGESTES**:

What a change!

**YDASAN**:

What a prodigy!

**YDACE**:

Happy day!

**ARGIDUS**:

Father, you astonish me; and perhaps in my turn

At this moment I am going to astonish you.

You deign to cede to me this brilliant diadem,

Inestimable prize of your warrior toil,

That your valiant hands covered with laurels.

I dare to accept from you this august share,

And before your eyes I am going to make a worthy use of it.

Plato came to these shores; he instructed kings;

My heart is his disciple; and I will follow his laws.

A sage instructed me, but it is you I am imitating.

Your example to live as a citizen invites me.

You are above all sovereign honors.

You trample them under your feet, lord, and I fear them.

Misfortune to any mortal who thinks himself capable

Of bearing this formidable weight after you!

People, I am using a moment of my authority.

I reign—your king returns your freedom to you.

(he descends the throne)

Agathocles just gave justice to his son;

I give it to all of you. May propitious heaven

From this day begin a century of happiness,

A century of virtue, rather than grandeur!

O my august spouse! O noble citizeness!

This people cherish you; you are more than queen.

**CURTAIN**

# THE DUKE OF ALENÇON

# CAST OF CHARACTERS

**THE DUKE OF ALENÇON (D'ALENÇON)**

**NEMOURS, his brother**

**LE SIRE DE COUCY**

**DANGESTE, brother of Adelaide de Guesclin**

**AN OFFICER**

# ACT I

*The action takes place in the town of De Lusignan, in Poitou.*

**COUCY:**

Lord, in arriving in this abode of dangers,

I am stealing a moment from the tumult of arms.

Brother of Adelaide, and like her committed

To the party of the Dauphin, by heaven protected,

You are seeing me thrown in the contrary role;

But I am your friend more than your adversary.

You were aware of my plans, you knew my heart.

You yourself had destined me for your sister.

But I must speak to you and make you understand

The soul of a true soldier, worthy of you, perhaps.

**DANGESTE:**

Lord, you can do anything.

**COUCY:**

My hands are bearing the standards

Of the Prince d'Alençon to the field of Mars.

I loved him in peace, I will serve him in war.

I am fighting for him alone and not for England.

In these frightful times of discord and horror,

I have no other role than that of my heart.

Not that for this hero my forewarned soul

Always intends to shut his faults from sight.

I am not blind; I see with sorrow

The indiscreet heat of his distractions.

I see that with his sense of impetuous intoxication

The abandonment to excess of a passionate youth.

And this impetuous torrent, that I stop with effort

Too often tears him from me, and carries him too far.

But he has virtues which redeem his vices.

Eh! Who knows, lord, where to place his services,

If we never failed to follow and cherish

Any but hearts without weakness and perfect princes?

All my blood is his; but in the end this sword

Regrets being soaked in French blood.

The generous dauphin—

**DANGESTE:**

Dare call him king.

**COUCY:**

Until today, lord, he wasn't for me.

It is true, I wanted to bring him my homage,

All my wishes are for him, but friendship engages me.

The Duke has my oaths; I cannot, today

Either serve, or treat or change, except with him.

The misfortunes of our times, our sinister discords,

The court abandoned to the intrigues of ministers,

All precipitated him into this role.

I cannot bend his will to my choice.

I have often, by his envenomed wounds

Revolted his pride with harsh truths.

Your sister could recall him to virtues,

Lord, and it's of that I am seeking to speak to you.

In more tranquil times I loved Adelaide,

Before when Lusignan was your happy asylum;

I thought that she might, approving my plan,

Accept without scorn my homage and my hand.

Soon she was carried off by these English.

To new destinies she was reserved.

What was I to do? Where was heaven directing my steps?

The Duke, more fortunate, saved her from their arms.

The glory of it is his, let him have the reward.

He has by too many rights deserved to please her.

He is prince, he is young, he is your avenger.

His good deeds and his name all speak in his favor.

Justice and love urge her to surrender.

I did not avenge her and I have no pretension.

I am silent.— Still, he must deserve her

Against all others except him, I would fight for her.

I would hardly give in to the children of the king himself.

But this prince is my chief; he cherishes me, I love him.

Coucy, neither virtuous nor brave by half,

Would have braved the prince and given way to his friend.

I do more: with my weak senses governed

I dare to support the tenderness of my rival.

To mark you your glory and what you owe

To heroes that you serve and through whom you live.

With a dry eye and unenvious heart I will see

This marriage which could poison my life.

I rejoin for you my service and my vows.

This arm, which was for him, will fight for the two of you.

Lover of Adelaide, noble and faithful friend,

Soldier of her spouse, and full of the same zeal,

I will serve under him, as it will be necessary one day

When I shall command, he will serve me in my turn.

Those are my feelings: if I have sacrificed myself,

Friendship directed me to do it, and especially the country.

Think that if the marriage places her under his sway,

If the prince serves her, he will serve the king.

**DANGESTE**:

Lord, how I contemplate you with astonishment!

What a rare and great example you give to the world!

What! This heart, I think it without dissimulation and evasion,

Knows only friendship and can brave love!

One must admire you, when one gets to know you;

You serve your friend; you will serve my master.

Such a generous heart must think like me;

All those of your blood are the support of their king;

But the fatal pursuit of the Duke d'Alençon—

(The Duke enters.)

**DUKE**:

(to Dangeste)

Is it she who's escaping me? Is it she who avoids me?

Dangeste, stay. You know too well

The sorrowful distractions of a heart such as mine.

You know if I love her, and if I've served her.

If I await a look for the destiny of my life,

Don't let her extend the excess of her power

To carry my passion to the last despair.

I hate these idle ceremonies, this gratitude

That her frigid timidity opposes to my constancy.

The slightest delay is a cruel refusal.

An affront that my heart will no longer pardon.

It's in vain that to France, to her faithful master,

She exposes to my eyes the splendor of her zeal.

I intend that all give way to my love, to me.

Let her find in me alone her country and her king.

She owes me her life and even her honor.

And as for me, I owe her everything, since it's I who love her.

Joined by so many rights, it's too much to separate us.

The altar is ready, I am rushing to it, go there to prepare it.

(Exit Dangeste.)

**COUCY**:

Lord, are you thinking indeed, that the destiny of the state

Depends on this day?

**DUKE**:

Yes, you will see me conquer, or die her spouse.

**COUCY**:

The Dauphin is advancing, and isn't far from us.

**DUKE**:

I'm waiting for him without fearing him,

And I'm going to fight him.

Do you think my weakness has been able to beat me down?

Do you think that love, my tyrant, my conqueror,

Has choked the ardor for glory in my soul?

If the ingrate hates me, I intend that she admire me.

No question she has a sovereign empire over me.

But not enough to wither my virtue.

Ah! Too severe friend, what, do you reproach me?

No, don't judge me with such injustice.

Is it some French man that love degrades?

Beloved lovers, happily, all go into battle,

And from the breast of happiness fly toward death.

I will die, worthy at least, of the ingrate that I love.

**COUCY**:

Rather, let my prince be worthy of himself.

The safety of the State concerns me today.

I speak to you of yours and you speak to me of love.

The Burgundians and the English in their sad alliance

Have excavated with our hands the tombs of France.

Your fate is doubtful. Your life prodigious.

For our real enemies who we subjugated

Think that it needs three hundred years of constancy

To attack by degrees this vast power.

The Dauphin is offering you an honorable peace.

**DUKE**:

No, from his favorites I will never have it.

Friend, I hate the English, but I hate more

These cowardly councilors whose favor outrages me.

This son of Charles VI, this odious court,

These insolent fops have embittered me without possibility of change.

My soul has been too much struck by their bloody affronts.

In a word, when I drew my sword against Charles,

It's not, dear Coucy, to place it at his feet,

To abase in his court our humiliated faces,

To serve in cowardice an arbitrary minister.

**COUCY**:

No, it's to obtain a necessary peace.

Eh! What other interest could you listen to?

**DUKE**:

The interest of a wrath that nothing can subdue.

**COUCY**:

You push love and anger to the extreme.

**DUKE**:

I know it; I haven't been able to soften my character.

**COUCY**:

You must, you can: I'm not flattering you.

But, in condemning you, I will follow all your steps.

One must show his injustice to his friend

To enlighten him, to stop him on the edge of a precipice.

I had to do it, I did it despite your wrath.

You insist on falling in, and I'm rushing after you.

**DUKE**:

Friend, what have you told me?

(An officer enters.)

**OFFICER**:

Lord, the assault is ready.

These walls are surrounded.

**COUCY**:

March at our head.

**DUKE**:

Friend, I am not in any pain to resist

The bold hands that come to insult me.

Of all the enemies that must still be fought

I fear only one, she's the one I adore.

**CURTAIN**

# ACT II

**THE DUKE:**

Victory is ours, your efforts assured it.

Your advice guided my distracted youth.

It's you whose precise mind and penetrating eyes

Watched in a hundred different places for my defense.

Why don't I have, like you, this calm courage,

So cold in danger, so calm in storms?

Coucy is necessary to me in council, in battles,

And it's up to his great soul to direct my arm.

**COUCY:**

Prince, this fiery warrior that they see appear in you

Will be master of all, when you are his master.

You've known how to rule and you've conquered.

Having at all times this useful virtue,

He who knows how to possess himself can command the world.

As for me, whose arm weakly seconded yours,

I knew my duty and I really followed it ill;

In the heat of combat I served you so little.

Our warriors marched to victory on your heels.

And to follow the Bourbons, that is to fly to glory.

The leader of the assailants storming our ramparts

Was by your valiant hands thrice hurled down,

Doubtless at the foot of the walls exhaling his fury.

And paid for this assault with the rest of his life.

**DUKE**:

Dear friend, who is this audacious chief,

Who, seeking death, hid from our eyes?

His helmet was closed: what inconceivable charm,

Even in combat made him respectable!

Is this the unique effect of his rare valor,

Which still imposes on me, and speaks in his favor?

While I was measuring my arms against him,

I felt, despite myself, new alarms.

And I don't know what trouble arose in me,

Be it this sad love to which I am captive

Over my distracted senses its tenderness spread

Even in the breast of battle it loaned me its weakness.

So that it seemed to mark all my actions

With the noble sweetness of its impressions.

Or be it the voice of my sad country

Speaking again in secret to the heart which betrayed it

Wherein the fatal dart was thrust into my heart

Corrupting at all times my glory and my happiness.

**COUCY:**

As for the darts whose power your soul has sensed,

All advice is vain: permit my silence.

But this French blood which our hands have shed,

But the State, the country, I must speak to you about it.

I foresee that soon this fatal war,

These intestine troubles of the royal house,

These sad factions will give way to danger

To abandon France to the foreign hands

Whose laws are odious, whose race is little loved.

We hate the usurper, we love the fatherland.

And the blood of the Capets is still adored.

Sooner or later it's necessary that this sacred throne,

Whose divided branches bent by the storm

More united and more beautiful are our sole shade.

You, situated near the throne, attached to this throne,

Though the misfortunes of the time have torn you away from it,

Have foreign connections that you must resolve;

Interest formed them, honor can dissolve them.

Such are my feelings that I cannot betray.

**DUKE**:

What! She still fears to present herself before my eyes!

What! When I submit my fortune at her knees,

Concealing myself from the shouts of an importunate crowd,

And the acclamations of soldiers that follow me,

I was seeking near her a happiness which flees me,

Adelaide still avoids my presence.

She insults my passion, my perseverance.

Her calm pride, producing its harshness,

Revels in my weakness and laughs at my sorrows!

Oh! If I believed it, if this too tender love—

**COUCY**:

Lord, it's time to return to my duty.

In your name, with assiduous efforts, I am going

To honor the conquerors, to comfort the vanquished,

To calm the disputes between your forces and the English.

Now those are your interests and I know no others.

**DUKE**:

You aren't listening to me, you are talking about duty

When my heart is pouring its despair into yours.

Go ahead then, fulfill the duties of which I am incapable.

Go, leave a wretch alone with the scorn which overwhelms him.

I am blushing before you, but without repenting,

I cherish my errors, and don't want to give them up.

Go, leave me alone, I tell you, to my profound sorrow.

The one I love flees me, and I flee the whole world.

Go, you condemn too much the distractions of my heart.

**COUCY**:

No, I pity your weakness and I fear the fury of it.

(Exit Coucy.)

**DUKE**:

(alone) O heaven! How happy he is, and how I envy

The free pride of that bold soul!

He sees without alarm, he sees without being dazzled,

The funereal beauty that I want to hate.

This imperious star which presides over my life,

Has neither fires nor rays that his eye doesn't challenge.

And as for me, I serve her in cowardice,

And I offer to her attractions

Vows that I detest, and that are not received!

Dangeste supports her and renders her more harsh.

How I hate the two of them! Let's flee the brother at least!

Let's leave there this captive that he's bringing hereabouts.

Except for Adelaide, all here wound my eyes.

(Exit Duke. Enter the Duke de Nemours, and Dangeste from a different direction.)

**NEMOURS**:

At last, after three years you see me again, Dangeste!

But in what parts, o heaven! In what funereal condition!

**DANGESTE**:

Your life's in peril and this agitated blood—

**NEMOURS**:

My deplorable life is very secure;

My wound is slight, and painless,

That of my heart is deep and terrible!

**DANGESTE**:

Give thanks to heaven that permitted

You to fall to such enemies and

Not under the terrible yoke of a foreign hand.

**NEMOURS**:

How hard it really is to be in the hands of his brother!

**DANGESTE**:

But raised together in happier times,

The most tender friendship united the two of you.

**NEMOURS**:

He used to love me, that's how it begins

But soon friendship flew off with infancy.

Ah! How the cruel one separated from me!

Faithless to the State, to nature, to king,

They say he's taken from a foreign race

The fierce pride and harsh character!

He doesn't know what he made me suffer.

And my heart is torn apart, not knowing how to hate him.

**DANGESTE**:

He doesn't suspect that he has in his power

An unfortunate brother who animates vengeance.

**NEMOURS:**

No. Vengeance, friend, doesn't enter my heart anymore.

What a different care distracts my valor!

Ah! Speak: is it really true what rumor

Announces in France to my disturbed soul?

Is it true that an illustrious, unfortunate creature,

A heart, alas! Too worthy of captivating his prayers,

Adelaide, at last, holds him in her power?

What do they say about it? What do you know of their relationship?

**DANGESTE:**

Prisoner like you in these odious walls,

These secret mysteries offend my sight.

And in any case, what I knew— But I see him appear.

**NEMOURS:**

O shame! O despair which I cannot master.

(Enter the Duke with his following.)

**DUKE:**

(to his suite) After having shown this rare valor

Can he still blush to have me for a conqueror?

He's turning away.

**NEMOURS**:

O fate! O funereal day

Which tears the rest from my sad life!

Into what hands, o heaven, has my misfortune delivered me!

**DUKE**:

What do I hear and what tone has struck my spirit!

**NEMOURS**:

Are you unable to recognize me?

**DUKE**:

Ah! Nemours, ah! My brother.

**NEMOURS**:

That name, formerly so dear, that name despairs me.

I know him too well, this unfortunate brother,

Your conquered enemy, your enchained captive.

**DUKE**:

You are no longer anything but my brother,

And my heart pardons you

But, I will confess it, your cruelty astonishes me

If your king pursues me, Nemours, was it up to you

To solicit, to fulfill this odious employment?

What have I done to you?

**NEMOURS**:

You are the misfortune of my life.

I wish that today your hand had ravished me.

**DUKE**:

What an unfortunate effect of our civil discontents!

**NEMOURS**:

The discontents of my heart are even more frightful.

**DUKE**:

I would have loved to display my courage against another.

Alas! How I pity you!

**NEMOURS**:

I pity you more

For hating your country, for betraying without remorse

Both the king who loved you and the blood you spring from.

**DUKE**:

Stop, spare me the infamy of the name of traitor

Perhaps at that unworthy word I would forget myself.

No, my brother, never have I less deserved

This odious reproach of infidelity.

I am ready to give to our sad provinces,

To bloody France, to the rest of our princes,

The august and holy example of reunion,

After having given it that of division.

**NEMOURS**:

You! You are capable—

**DUKE**:

This day, which seemed so funereal,

Will extinguish the remaining flames of discord.

**NEMOURS**:

This day is too horrible!

**DUKE:**

It's going to complete my wishes.

**NEMOURS**:

What do you mean?

**DUKE**:

Everything is changed, your brother is too happy.

**NEMOURS**:

I believe you; they said that with an intense love,

Violent, frantic, for that's the way you love,

Your heart has been occupied for the entire last three months?

**DUKE**:

I love, yes, fame has published it.

Yes, I love with fury: such an alliance

Seemed to be waiting for your presence for my happiness.

Yes, my resentment, my rights, my allies,

Glory, friends, enemies, I am placing them all at her feet.

(to his suite)

Go, and tell her that these two wretched brothers,

Hurled by destiny into contrary factions,

Are going to march henceforth under the same standard and

Are only waiting for a glance from her sovereign eyes.

(to Nemours)

Don't blame any further the love to which your brother is prey.

To justify myself, it suffices that you see her.

**NEMOURS**:

(aside) Cruel! (to Duke) She loves you!

**DUKE**:

At least she owes me it.

It was only an obstacle to the success of my plans.

It no longer is: I intend that nothing separate us.

**NEMOURS**:

(aside)

What terrible blows the cruel one is preparing for me!

(aloud) Listen! Are you only going to insult my sorrow?

Do you know me? Do you know what I dared to attempt?

In this funereal place, do you know what brought me?

**DUKE**:

Let's forget these subjects of discord and hate.

And you, my brother, and you, be witness here

If the excess of love can carry further!

What you condemn, or rather your prayer,

The generous Coucy, the king, the whole of France,

Are all demanding together, and they couldn't obtain it.

Submissive and subjugated, I am offering it to her attractions.

(to Dangeste)

You feared the homage of the enemy of kings.

You love, you serve a court that outrages me.

Well! It's necessary to give in. Dispose of me.

I no longer have allies, I am your king's.

Love which, despite you, made us for each other

Leaves me no choice but your side.

You, run, my dear brother, go at this moment

To announce to the court such a great change.

Be free; leave and of my sacrifices

Go offer to the king the happy fruits.

Would I were able today to present at his knees

She who has subdued me, who is bringing me to him,

Who of an enemy prince has made a faithful subject,

Changed by her looks, and virtuous through her!

**NEMOURS**:

(aside) He's doing what I want and it's ruining me.

(aloud) O too cruel brother!

**DUKE**:

What do I hear?

**NEMOURS**:

I must speak.

**DUKE**:

What do you wish to tell me? And why such alarms?

You don't know her formidable charms.

**NEMOURS:**

Heaven is placing an eternal obstacle between us.

**DUKE**:

Between us—that's too much. Cruel, what have you said?

But of you, indeed, was she unaware?

Heaven! To what frightful trap will my honor be delivered!

Tremble!

**NEMOURS**:

As for me, how I tremble! Ah! I've devoured too much

The inexpressible horror in which you alone have delivered me.

I've kept my distractions silent too long.

Know me, then, barbarian, and take your vengeance.

Know a despair equal to your furors.

Strike! Behold my heart, and behold your rival!

**DUKE**:

You, cruel one! You, Nemours!

**NEMOURS**:

Yes, for the last two years

The most secret love has joined our fates.

It's you whose furors have tried to tear from me

The sole blessing on earth I've been able to attach to me.

For the last three months you've made my life horrors.

The ills that I've experienced surpass your jealousy.

From your distraction, judge my exaltation.

The two of us borrow from this blood I came from

The excess of passions that devour the soul.

Nature has given us both a heart all aflame.

My brother is my rival and I fought him.

I silenced blood, perhaps virtue.

Furious, blind, more jealous than yourself

I rushed, I flew, to separate you from the one I love.

Nothing held me back, neither your superb towers

Nor the few soldiers I had for aid.

Nor the time, nor the place, nor even your courage.

I saw only my flame and your passion which outraged me.

The only thing more I will tell you about this, without this same love

I would, to serve you, willingly lose my life.

So that, if you succumbed to your contrary destiny,

You would find in me the most tender of brothers.

Let Nemours, who loves you, be sacrificed for you.

Everything in the whole world, except her and my king.

I don't wish in cowardliness to appease your vengeance.

I am your enemy, I am in your power.

In my heart love was stronger than friendship.

Be cruel like me, punish me without pity.

As well, you can assure yourself of your conquest,

You cannot marry her except at the price of my head.

In the face of the heavens, I give you my word,

I make you the witness of our vows against yourself.

Strike, so that after the blow, your jealous cruelty

Drags to the foot of the altars, your sister and my spouse!

Strike, I tell you: do you dare?

**DUKE**:

Traitor, that's enough of that.

Soldiers, let him be removed from my sight: obey!

(Coucy enters.)

**COUCY:**

I was going to leave, Lord, a bold populace

Is rising in tumult in the name of your brother.

The disorder is everywhere. Your confused soldiers

Are deserting the flags of their astonished chiefs.

And to complete the ills, the enemy is reassembling

To march its army on the alarmed city.

**DUKE:**

Go, cruel brother, go! You won't revel

In the fruit of your hate and your attempts.

Go back in. I am going to display their master to the factious.

Dangeste, follow me. (to Coucy) You watch over this traitor.

(Exit the Duke and his suite.)

**COUCY:**

Can it be you, Lord? Would you have given the lie

To the blood of the heroes from which you come?

Would you have violated by this cowardly insult

The laws of war and those of nature?

Could a prince forget himself to this degree?

**NEMOURS**:

No, but am I reduced to justifying myself?

Coucy, this populace is just, it's teaching you to know

That my brother is a rebel, and that Charles is his master.

**COUCY**:

Listen: that would be the fulfillment of my wishes,

To be able to reunite the two of you today.

With regret I see France desolated,

Nature sacrificed to our dissensions

The English, raising themselves greatly on our common ruin,

Threatening this state that we ourselves have weakened.

If you have a heart worthy of your race

Let your disgrace serve the public welfare.

Bring the parties together: join yourself with me

To calm your brother and appease your king,

To extinguish the fire of our civil wars.

**NEMOURS**:

Don't flatter yourself about that: your efforts are useless.

If discord alone had raised my arm,

If war and hate had guided my steps,

You could hope to reunite two brothers,

Each taking a contrary side.

A greater obstacle opposes itself to this reversal.

**COUCY**:

And what is that, Lord?

**NEMOURS**:

Ah! Recognize love,

Recognize the fury which carries both of us away

Which made me bold and renders him barbarous.

**COUCY**:

Must heaven see this? The fruit of the most noble plans

Annihilated by idle caprices.

Love to conquer all cruelly weakens

Blood which revolts to choke the tenderness

Of brothers who hate each other, and gives birth in all climes

To great passions: the misfortune of States!

Prince, let's leave there the mystery of your loves.

I pity the two of you, but I serve your brother.

I am going to second him; I am going to join myself to him

Against an insolent populace, which is making itself your support.

The most pressing danger is the one which calls me.

I see that it can have one quite cruel ending.

I see passions more powerful than myself.

And love alone makes me shiver here with terror.

But the prince is waiting for me;

I am leaving you, and I am flying there.

Be my prisoner, but on your word.

That suffices me.

**NEMOURS**:

I give it.

**COUCY**:

And as for me,

I would wish that this step brought his to the king.

In the passion for pleasing, I would like to cement

A union so precious with the blood of our tyrants,

But these proud enemies are indeed less dangerous

Than this fatal love which will ruin the two of you.

**CURTAIN**

# ACT III

**NEMOURS**:

No, no, this populace is arming itself in vain to defend me.

My brother, stained with blood, intoxicated with vengeance,

Became more jealous, more proud, and more cruel,

Dragging his victim to the altar before my eyes.

I didn't come to dispute my conquest

Just to be witness to this horrible celebration?

And in the despair into which I feel myself plunged,

By her flight at least my heart can be avenged.

Just heaven!

**DANGESTE**:

Ah! Lord, where have you taken her?

What! You are abandoning her, you direct her flight!

She cannot leave except by following her spouse.

Leave me alone to confront the prince's wrath.

**NEMOURS**:

Prisoner on my oath, in the horror which is urging me,

I am more enchained by my sole promise

Than by the heavy fetters

That the inhuman tyrants of this state could impose.

Honor delivers me to the power of my brother.

I can die for her and I cannot follow her.

She's already been escorted by obscure paths

That will soon free her from these guilty walls.

Love joined us and now love separates us.

**DANGESTE**:

Still, you remain in the power of a barbarian.

Lord, the English are thirsty for your blood.

Is this blood still sacred to your brother?

Fear that he may grant, in his funereal wrath,

To the allies he loves, a rival that he detests.

**NEMOURS:**

He wouldn't dare.

**DANGESTE:**

His heart knows no check.

He threatened you: does he threaten idly?

**NEMOURS:**

He will soon tremble: the king is coming and will avenge us.

Half of this populace are falling in with his flags.

Don't fear anything, friend. Heaven! What a frightful tumult!

(Enter the Duke and guards.)

**DUKE:**

I hear him. It's himself. Stop, wretch!

Coward who's betraying me, unworthy rival, stop!

**NEMOURS:**

He didn't betray you, but he's offering you his head.

Show to all the excess of your hate and your fury.

Go, don't waste time; heaven is arming itself as an avenger.

Tremble, your king is approaching, he's coming, he's going to appear.

You only conquered me: beware still, your master.

**DUKE**:

He can avenge you, but he cannot succor you;

And your blood—

**DANGESTE**:

No, cruel one, it's up to me to die.

I did everything, it's by me your guard was seduced.

I won over your soldiers, I prepared her flight.

Punish such great attempts and crimes

For escaping slavery and for fleeing her tyrants.

But respect your brother, his wife, and yourself.

He didn't betray you, he's a brother who loves you.

He wants to serve you when you want to oppress him.

Is it up to you to punish when the crime is love?

**DUKE**:

Let the two of them be guarded: go, let me be obeyed.

Go, I say: their sight increases my torture.

**NEMOURS**:

Cruel one; I know the passions of our blood.

In us all the passions are furors.

I expect death from you; but, even in my misfortune,

I am sufficiently avenged:

She hates you and she loves me.

(Exit Dangeste and Nemours.)

**THE DUKE**:

She loves you and you are going to die!

How many horrors at once!

Love, unworthy love, you've ruined all three of us!

**COUCY**:

He no longer knows himself, he's succumbing to his rage.

**DUKE**:

Well! Would you suffer my shame and my outrage?

Time presses: do you want an odious rival

To carry off the faithless one and marry her in front of my eyes?

You are afraid to answer me. Would you wait until the traitor

Has raised my populace and delivered me to his master?

**COUCY:**

I see clearly the effect the role of the king has

In these weary hearts in making faith waver.

The flame of sedition quelled

Is still alive, in hearts in secret reignited,

Believe me, sooner or later we'll see rejoined

The scattered debris of the French Empire.

The standards of France have appeared in the plain.

And you will be ruined if this agitated people

Believe treason to be safe.

Your dangers are growing.

**DUKE:**

Cruel one, what must be done?

**COUCY:**

Prevent them; subdue love and its wrath.

My prince, in this extremity let's still have

The strength to take a sure role.

We can conjure or brave the tempest,

Whatever you decide, my hand is always ready.

You wanted, this morning, with a happy treaty

To appease with glory an irritated monarch.

Don't be discouraged; direct, and I hope

To sign this salutary peace in your name.

But if you must fight and rush to death,

You know that a friend will not survive you.

**DUKE**:

Friend, leave me to descend to the tomb alone.

Live to serve my cause, and to avenge my ashes.

My destiny is accomplished, and I rush to be over with it.

He who really seeks death is sure to find it.

But I want it to be terrible, and when I succumb,

I want to see my rival dragged into my tomb.

**COUCY**:

What do you mean! With what horror are you possessed?

**DUKE**:

He is in this tower where you alone command.

**COUCY**:

What! Your brother?

**DUKE**:

Him? Is Nemours my brother?

He braves my love, he braves my wrath,

He's delivering me to his master; he alone oppressed me.

He caused my people to rise; still he is loved.

In one day he commits all crimes against me!

Share my furious rages; they are legitimate.

You alone, after my death, will reap the fruit.

The head of these English introduced into the town

Demands in the name of his people the head of a perjurer.

**COUCY**:

You've promised them to betray nature?

**DUKE**:

They've proscribed the blood of the faithless one for a long while.

**COUCY**:

And to obey them you will pierce his flank?

**DUKE**:

No, I won't obey their foreign hate.

I am obeying my rage and intend to satisfy it.

Does it matter to me whether it be the State or my vain allies?

**COUCY**:

So, then you are sacrificing him to love,

And you charge, me, me with his death!

**DUKE**:

I wasn't expecting this prompt justice from you.

I am truly wretched, really worthy of pity.

Betrayed in my love, betrayed in my friendship.

Ah! Too lucky Dauphin, it's your fate that I envy.

At least your friendship has never been betrayed.

And when you were offended, Tangui du Chatel

Served you without scruple and without hesitating.

**COUCY:**

He paid dearly for that terrible sacrifice.

**DUKE**:

Mine will cost more, but I wish this service.

Yes, I insist on it. My death will follow it instantly.

But, at least, my rival will perish before me.

Go, in the fate that presses me, I can still

Find friends who will keep their promise.

Others will serve me and won't urge

The excuse of ingrates, that sad virtue.

**COUCY:**

(after a long silence)

No, I've chosen my role, be it crime, be it justice,

You shall not complain that a friend betrayed you.

I deliver myself, not you, not to your furor,

But to other reasons which speak to my heart.

I see that it is time for extreme measures

That the most holy duties can silence themselves.

I won't allow you to test the fidelity

Of someone other than myself in such moments.

And you will recognize, by the success of my zeal,

If Coucy loved you, and if he was loyal.

(Exit Coucy.)

**DUKE**:

No, his frigid friendship won't serve me.

No, I have no friends: all hearts are ingrates.

(to a soldier)

Listen, go to the tower diligently.

(speaking low to him)

You understand: fly and serve my vengeance.

My heart counted too much on the uncertain Coucy.

He saw my furor with calm.

One doesn't comfort sorrows that one scorns.

It is necessary that my vengeance be placed in other hands.

You, that on our ramparts carry our flags,

Let them prepare for new perils.

(soldiers leave)

Well! So that's the end of it: a perfidious woman

Is leading me to the tomb charged with parricide!

Who, me, I will tremble at the blows to come!

I cherish vengeance and cannot taste it.

I shiver, a voice quaking and severe

Is crying in the depths of my heart.

Stop: he is your brother!

Ah! Unfortunate prince, mired in your hate,

Think of more holy laws. Nemours was your friend.

O days of our childhood! O past tendernesses!

He was the confidant of all my thoughts.

With what innocence and what effusions

Our hearts experienced their first feelings!

How many times, sharing my burgeoning alarms,

Did he dry my tears with a fraternal hand!

And it's I who am sacrificing him, and that same hand

Of a brother that I loved, will tear him apart.

Funereal passion whose madness distracts me,

No, I wasn't born to become barbarous.

I feel what a cruel weight the crime is—

But, what am I saying? Nemours is the only criminal?

I recognize my blood, but it's his fury;

He is carrying off the creature on whom my life depends.

He loves Adelaide— Ah! Too jealous distraction.

He loves her; is that a felony deserving of death?

But he himself, he attacks me, he braves my wrath.

He deceives me, he hates me— Never mind, he is my brother.

It's for him alone to love: he living, he is happy,

It's up to me to die, but let's die generous.

I haven't heard the homicidal signal,

The organ of felonies, the voice of parricide.

There is still time.

(An officer enters.)

Let everything be suspended.

Fly to the tower.

**OFFICER**:

Lord—

**DUKE**:

What are you alarmed by?

Heaven! You are weeping.

**OFFICER**:

I saw, not far from this door,

A body stained with blood that was being carried in secret.

It was Coucy who directed it and I fear the fate that—

**DUKE**:

(cannon fire can be heard)

What! Already! What do I hear? Ah! Heaven! My brother is dead!

He is dead! And I'm alive, and the earth is opening up

And lightning hasn't avenged his ruin!

Enemy of the state, factious, inhuman,

Unnatural brother, ravisher, assassin,

O heaven! I've dug out abysses around me.

How love has changed me, how many crimes it has cost me!

The veil is torn away, I knew myself ill.

I've arrived at the summit of felonies!

Ah, Nemours! Ah, my brother! Ah, day of my ruin!

I know that you loved me, and my arm assassinated you!

My brother!

**OFFICER:**

Lord, Adelaide urgently

Wishes to speak with you in secret for a moment.

**DUKE:**

Dear friend, prevent the cruel one from coming.

I can neither sustain nor endure her presence.

I don't deserve to perish before her eyes.

(drawing his sword)

Tell her that my blood—

**COUCY:**

(entering) What furious distractions!

**DUKE:**

Let me alone to punish myself and give myself up to justice.

(to Coucy)

What! You are made the accomplice in an assassination.

Minister of my crime, did you obey me?

**COUCY**:

Lord, I had promised to serve you.

**DUKE**:

Wretch that I am! Your rough severity

Combated the weakness of my hand a hundred times.

Did you have to give in to my sad wishes

When my passion directed you to crimes?

You obeyed me only to destroy my brother!

**COUCY**:

Had I refused this bloody ministry,

Your blind wrath wasn't swiftly

Going to charge another hand with the care of avenging you?

**DUKE**:

Love, only love, always master of my feelings,

By separating me from my reason would perhaps have excused me.

But you, whose wisdom and reflections

Have calmed all passions in your breast,

You whose firm and rigid mind I'd often feared,

Calmly permitted a parricide!

**COUCY**:

Well! Since shame and repentance

By which virtue speaks to those able to betray it

With such just remorse—has penetrated your soul,

Because despite the excess of your blind passion

At the price of your blood you wanted to save,

This blood that your madness wanted to deprive you of,

I can in that case explain myself. I can in that case inform you

That Coucy knew in the end how to protect you from yourself.

Know yourself, Lord, and calm your sorrows.

(Dangeste enters)

(to Dangeste)

But keep your remorse and dry your tears,

Let this day be salutary to all three of you.

Come, appear, prince, embrace your brother!

(Nemours appears.)

**DANGESTE**:

Lord—

**DUKE**:

My brother—

**DANGESTE**:

Ah! Heaven!

**DUKE**:

What could he have thought?

**NEMOURS**:

(coming forward to the middle of the stage)

I dare yet to see you again, to pity you, and to embrace you.

**DUKE**:

My crime is even greater since your heart forgot it.

**DANGESTE**:

Coucy, worthy hero, who gave him life.

**DUKE**:

He gave it to all three of us.

**COUCY**:

An unworthy assassin,

Before my eyes, raised his hand against Nemours.

I struck down the barbarian, and still foreseeing

The blind madness of the passion which is devouring you,

I made them swiftly give the odious signal,

Certain that in time your eyes would be opened.

**DUKE**:

After this grand example and this exemplary service

The reward that I owe you is to make myself worthy of you.

**NEMOURS**:

The two of us would like to serve you next to the king.

What is your plan? Speak.

**DUKE**:

To punish myself,

To surrender all three of us to an equal justice.

To expiate before you, by the greatest sacrifice,

The greatest of crimes in which the fatality

Of love and wrath precipitated me.

I loved Adelaide and my cruel passion

Is again stirring itself up for her in my desolated heart.

Coucy knew to what degree I adore her attractions

When my jealous rage ordered your death.

Still persecuted by the fire that possesses me

I adore her yet more, and my heart gives in to her.

I'm tearing my heart out by making you happy;

Love each other, but at least the two of you forgive me.

**NEMOURS**:

Ah! Your brother at your feet, worthy of your clemency,

Equals your blessings by his gratitude.

**DANGESTE**:

Yes, Lord, with him I embrace your knees.

The most tender friendship is going to rejoin me to you.

You are paying us too well for the sorrows we've suffered.

**DUKE:**

Ah! It's too much to display to me my misfortunes and my losses.

But you've all taught me to follow virtue.

My heart has not surrendered piecemeal.

(to Nemours)

I am your brother in everything; and my softened soul

Imitates your example and cherishes its fatherland.

Let's go inform the king, for whom you battled,

Of my crime, my remorse, and your happiness,

Yes, I wish to equal your faith, your zeal,

Towards blood, country, to faithful friendship.

And make you forget after so many torments

All my distractions through the strength of virtues.

**CURTAIN**

# THE TWO WINE CASKS

# CAST OF CHARACTERS

**GLYCERA**

**PRESTINE, little sister of Glycera**

**DAPHNIS**

**FATHER OF DAPHNIS**

**FATHER OF GLYCERA**

**GRÉGOIRE, priest of the temple of Bacchus, tavern-keeper/cook**

**PHEBE, a female servant of the temple**

**TROOPS of Young Men and Young Women**

*The action takes place in a temple dedicated to Bacchus.*

# ACT I

*The stage represents a temple with leaves, decorated with thyrus, shells, vine branches, grapes. Between columns of foliage statues of Bacchus, Ariane, Silenus, and Pan are seen. A huge buffet is placed before the altar; two fountains of wine spout in the background. Young lads and girls are hurrying to prepare everything for a celebration. Grégoire, one of the servants of Bacchus, is preparing the feast. He's in a white and elegant jacket, carrying a thyrus in his hand and wearing a crown of ivy on his head.*

*A gay and sprightly overture; refrain, sad and terrible.*

**GRÉGOIRE**:

(singing)

Come on children, strive with each other.

Young bachelors, young bachelorettes,

Adorn this glorious altar.

Bestir yourselves, lazy creatures that you are.

Put this there,

Make this buffet tidy,

Think what you're doing.

Come on children, strive with each other;

Bestir yourselves, lazies, that you are;

Think that you are serving beauties and the gods.

**A SERVING GIRL**:

(speaking)

Eh! Take it easy, Mr. Grégoire,

We are like you, of the temple of Bacchus.

Like you, we are making him glorious.

We are all very assiduous

To serve Venus and Bacchus.

The high priest of the temple is, no question, gone to drink.

(singing)

He will come back; act less important,

'Cause when the master's away,

Master's valet holds sway.

**GRÉGOIRE:**

Pardon, I am fretful.

**SERVING GIRL:**

None of that here.

You are making fun of us.

**GRÉGOIRE:**

Go, I've really got some worries.

We are awaiting the wedding, and my master ordered me

To take his place,

And to join the lovers who will be sent

From all the adjoining regions to be married.

Ah! I'm furious.

**SERVING GIRL:**

What! This is the best piece of luck

That you could ever find:

These celebrations are always worth some gift to us.

Nothing better could happen to you.

I've seen more than one marriage.

One party or the other

Repents often enough

The actions taken here.

But the gentleman who marries them,

Once he has their money, never repents of it.

It's the lovable Daphnis, and the beautiful Glycera,

Who are coming to give their hands to each other.

How charming Daphnis is!

**GRÉGOIRE**:

(wrathfully) No, he's very villainous.

**SERVING GIRL**:

How Daphnis has known how to please all our beauties!

**GRÉGOIRE:**

He greatly displeases me.

**SERVING GIRL**:

How handsome he is!

**GRÉGOIRE**:

How ugly he is!

**SERVING GIRL:**

Very honest lad, free-spender.

**GRÉGOIRE:**

No.

**SERVING GIRL:**

Is too!

How mean Grégoire is! Will you be telling me

That the intended is lacking in beauty?

**GRÉGOIRE:**

The intended?

**SERVING GIRL:**

Yes, Glycera. They celebrate her, they adore her.

All Arcadia is enchanted with her.

**GRÉGOIRE:**

Yes, the intended passes muster—she is pretty;

But she has a bad heart,

Completely full of perfidy, ingratitude, and pride.

**SERVING GIRL**:

Glycera, a bad heart! Alas, she's goodness,

She's modest virtue, and full of complacency.

She's sweetness, patience,

And the purity of her morals

Silences even slander.

You seem spiteful to me.

Did you ever attempt

To pinch the beauty's heart?

By success one is flattered;

If the lady is not cruel.

You treat her as nymph and divinity.

If you are rebuffed,

You compose songs against her.

Come on, Master Grégoire, a bit less wrath.

Let's give a good reception to these two spouses.

Let the banquet be magnificent.

They are drinking unwatered wine here;

But don't go spoil our bacchic feast

By breaking open bad wine casks.

**GRÉGOIRE**:

Huh? What are you saying there?

**SERVING GIRL**:

I understand myself perfectly.

**GRÉGOIRE**:

Little girl,

Tremble as this mystery may be revealed;

It's the secret of the gods, beware not to repeat it

As soon as it is told.

Learn that one dies the death quickly.

Cease your over-free speeches,

Contain your cursed tongue,

And respect the gods and their innkeepers.

(sings)

Come on, resume your work.

Indeed, let's serve these lucky lovers.

(aside)

Scorn and rage

Are tearing my feelings apart.

Let's hasten these lucky moments;

Courage, courage,

Beat, knock, all together now.

(the servants beat their hammers on copper castings that are used as ornaments)

Hang these festoons, spread these leaves;

Let these fine grapes, little cupids

Forever give us

Happy nights and fine days

Under these charming shadows.

I'm furious,

Furious,

I'll get even,

I'll punish them.

They'll pay me dearly for my outrage.

Let's hasten their happy moments.

Beat, knock, all together now.

I am furious,

Furious.

**SERVING GIRL**:

Ah! I notice this wedding party

On the road in the distance.

Glycera's little sister

Is always in the lead.

She's up really early;

That rose is already in flower.

She's rushed her steps.

Here she is—wouldn't you say

She's the one getting married?

**PRESTINE**:

(rushing in hastily) Eh! What's going on!

Is nothing ready in the temple of Bacchus?

We remain tongue tied! Have our steps been wasted?

They're doing nothing here when there's so much to do!

My sister and her lover, my jolly father,

And Daphnis, too, women, girls and lads,

Are filing in, dancing and singing,

And here I see nothing visible.

Reply, Grégoire, reply.

Take me to the altar and to milord, the high priest.

**GRÉGOIRE**:

I'm the high priest.

**PRESTINE**:

You're joking.

**GRÉGOIRE**:

I am, I say.

**PRESTINE**:

You? You, priest of Bacchus?

**GRÉGOIRE**:

And made for the job. What astonishment is yours?

**PRESTINE**:

Well! So be it; I'd prefer it to be you than someone else.

**GRÉGOIRE**:

I am vice manager in this attractive spot.

I join lovers and I fix their meals.

These two charming functions,

So necessary to the world,

Are no question the first.

I hope someday, my little Prestine,

To exercise them for you

In this hallowed dwelling.

**PRESTINE**:

Alas! Very willingly.

**(DUO) GRÉGOIRE AND PRESTINE:**

In these beautiful parts, it's up to Grégoire;

It's up to him to instruct

In the fine art of loving and drinking;

It's he who must reign.

From mighty god the vermillion liquor comes;

The temple is a cabaret;

His altar is a buffet.

Love awakes there

With delight;

Love sleeps there,

Sleeps, sleeps,

Under the beautiful trellised grapes.

**GRÉGOIRE**:

I see our people coming;

Right now I'm going to assume

My ceremonial robes.

Grégoire must justify to all eyes

The choice they made of him on this brilliant day.

**PRESTINE**:

Go quick. Come forward father, father-in-law,

My adored sister, my dear brother-in-law,

Ah! How slowly you walk.

They say this grave appearance is decent.

It's noble, it's graceful;

But in your place,

I'd move a little faster.

(Glycera's father and Daphnis' father, little old geezers shriveled up, come in first, cane in hand, then Daphnis escorting Glycera and all the wedding party.)

**GLYCERA**:

(to Prestine)

Dear sister, excuse my dazzled senses.

I stopped to look at Daphnis,

I was beside myself in ecstasy, in delirium;

And I had only one feeling;

Go, all I can tell you,

Is that I wish you the same.

**(DUO) THE TWO FATHERS:**

Oh, how sweet it is, in our old age,

To be reborn in our family!

My son— My daughter,

Revive my languishing age;

My winter shines

With roses of their youth.

Young folks, who want to have a laugh,

Treat old geezers

As dreamers and babblers.

They're very wrong;

Each aspires

To his fate.

Each demands of nature

To die only with grey hair;

And that those who make a hundred

Be remembered in the papers.

**PRESTINE**:

It's indeed a question of humming;

Ah! I think you have enough other business.

Do you know to what man they intend to give

The duty of celebrating your amorous mysteries?

To Grégoire.

**GLYCERA:**

(terrified) To Grégoire!

**DAPHNIS:**

Eh! What do I care, great god!

All is good to me, all is precious;

Everything's the same here if my happiness approaches.

If Glycera is mine, all the rest is foreign.

What matter the time

When I hear the time for surrender?

Nothing can displease me, and nothing interests me:

I don't see these games, this solemn meal,

These priests of Marriage, this temple, this altar.

I only see the goddess.

**QUARTET: THE TWO FATHERS, DAPHNIS, GLYCERA:**

Daughter! / My dear son! / Glycera! / My tender spouse!

Let's all four love each other, love ourselves.

Bright dawn be born of bliss,

Be born, be hatched,

An even sweeter day.

Tender love, it's you that I implore,

In all times you reign over us.

Tender love, it's you that I implore,

Let's all four love each other, love ourselves.

**PRESTINE**:

They love to sing and that's their folly.

Don't I get to take part?

At the drop of a hat, these folks form a quartet.

And I revere and admire 'em for it,

But they sing, sometimes, having nothing to say.

At the drop of a hat, they form a quartet.

It's very pleasing to my ear,

And if they asked me, I'd have made it a quintet.

But they left me here, just thinking of themselves.

(sings)

The first husband that I will have,

Ah! Great gods how I will sing.

I'll neglect myself,

I'll abandon myself.

The first husband I shall have,

Ah! Great gods, how I will sing!

**PHEBE**:

(entering) Come inside, my handsome gentlemen,

My beautiful lady.

(to Glycera aside)

My beautiful lady, at least be careful.

**DAPHNIS**:

Go, I will care for her, fear nothing, my good woman.

(places a purse in her hand)

**PHEBE**:

What two charming spouses we've got here!

Watch out for yourself carefully, madam.

**GLYCERA**:

What do you intend to tell me? She makes me tremble.

Love is very timid, and my heart is very tender.

**PRESTINE**:

With your lover nearby, what can bother you?

No fear in that case would grip me.

(sings)

The first husband I shall have,

Ah! Good gods, how I will sing!

I'll neglect myself,

I'll let myself go.

The first husband I shall have,

Ah! Great gods, how I will sing!

                    **CURTAIN**

# ACT II

*Daphnis escorted by his father, Glycera by hers, followed by Prestine, leave the temple and run about, also the young men of the wedding.*

**DAPHNIS' FATHER:**

Children, believe me, we know the ropes.

Doing as our very prudent ancestors did.

Everything was better then.

Those were the good times, and the ancient centuries,

Being older than we are, were always right.

I tell you that—here lad—will be—

Here—the girl; here—me, father of the lad.

· (to Glycera)

There you; and then Prestine over here by her sister,

To learn her part and know how to perform it well.

But I notice that the high-priest is ready.

What a grand and noble air he has!

A majestic holiness is imprinted on an august face.

He resembles his god, whose complexion he has.

**GLYCERA'S FATHER**:

Yes, it's plain he's served with great fervor.

Silence, listen carefully.

(Grégoire enters, followed by the priests of Bacchus. The two lovers put their hands on the buffet which serves as an altar. Grégoire is dressed as high priest.)

**GRÉGOIRE**:

Intended, and you, intended,

Who come to light at the altar of Bacchus,

The most beautiful flame and the purest ardor,

Be very welcome here.

First of all, before each swears

To observe the rites received,

Before creating the conjugal union,

I am going to present to you the nuptial bowl.

**GLYCERA:**

These rites are to love; what needs an oath

To fulfill a duty so precious and so long-lasting?

This oath is constantly in my heart, unalterably

Written in feelings

And unerasable characters.

Alas! If you like, my mouth will do it a hundred times.

I will repeat them every day of my life.

And don't think the number would bore me;

They will be all for my lover.

**GRÉGOIRE:**

(aside) How the happiness of these two increases my fury!

Gods! Let them be punished. Drink, beautiful Glycera,

And drink love in long draughts.

Drink, tender spouses, you will swear later.

You are receiving from the gods infinite favors.

(he goes to take the two cups prepared at the back of the buffet)

**DAPHNIS' FATHER**:

Yes, our fathers drank in their ceremonies.

They were worth more than ours are today.

After one no longer drinks, boredom makes

The best companies yawn.

Songs in refrains of dining are banished;

I used to laugh; I was always happy

And I no longer laugh since I got old;

I'm trying to find the reason;

What do you think is the cause, old pal?

**GLYCERA'S FATHER**:

Why—it comes—with time. I am very serious,

Quite often, despite myself, without knowing the cause;

It makes a change amongst us.

But there remain, after all, some touching pleasures.

The soul breathes easily in the happiness of others,

And when we marry our adorable children,

I see we are happy without laughing.

(Grégoire presents a small cup to Daphnis and another to Glycera.)

**GRÉGOIRE**:

(after they've drunk)

Return the cup to me. What! You are shivering.

There, swear now, you, Daphnis, begin.

**DAPHNIS**:

(singing a measured refrain, nobly and tenderly)

I swear by the gods, and especially by Glycera,

To love her forever as I love her this day.

All the flames of love

Have spread through this wine

As I emptied my cup.

O you, who deserved Ariane's heart,

Divine Bacchus, charming conqueror,

You reign over meals, loves, and war.

Divine Bacchus, charming conqueror,

I invoke you after my Glycera.

(Symphony)

Descend, Bacchus, to these beautiful abodes;

Bring the mother of cupids,

Bring with you all the gods;

They can burn for Glycera;

I won't be jealous of them.

Her heart prefers me,

Prefers me, prefers me—to the gods.

**GRÉGOIRE**:

It's your turn to swear, Glycera,

Before Bacchus himself, to the great god of love.

**GLYCERA**

(sings) I swear an implacable hate,

To this villainous ape,

To this dummy, this sot;

I find him insupportable,

I swear an implacable hate,

To this dummy, this sot.

Yes, father, yes, father,

I would much prefer

To marry Lucifer in hell.

Don't aggravate my rage further.

Yes, I'd rather see the few charms I have

In the mug of the dog Cerebus,

Than between the arms

Of this villain who thinks to please me.

**DAPHNIS**:

What have I heard! Great gods!

**THE TWO FATHERS:**

(together) Ah! My daughter!

**PRESTINE**:

Ah! My sister!

**GLYCERA**:

(recoiling) Ah! The horror!

Get out of my sight! Your very aspect afflicts me!

**DAPHNIS**:

What! This is the real you?

**GLYCERA**:

Withdraw, I tell you:

You'll give me the vapors.

**DAPHNIS**:

Eh! What's happening?

Powerful gods, vengeful gods,

Are you so jealous?

Are you separating me from the one I love?

My charming mistress, idol of my senses,

Come back to yours, get hold of yourself.

See Daphnis at your feet, eyes filled with tears.

**GLYCERA**:

I cannot abide you. I think I told you that.

Plainly enough, clearly enough.

Leave or I'm leaving.

**DAPHNIS' FATHER**:

Are you trying to test me

By these frightful vexations?

Did you intend to jest with my profound sorrow?

**GLYCERA:**

You won't go; I'm leaving;

I'd go to the ends of the earth to be far from you.

(she leaves)

**QUARTET: THE TWO FATHERS, PRESTINE, DAPHNIS**

I am completely confused. / I tremble. / I'm dying.

(all together)

What an alteration! What dangers!

Is this the marriage so sweet, so full of charms?

**PRESTINE:**

No, I will no longer laugh; flow, flow, my tears.

(all together)

Powerful god, give us your favors.

**GRÉGOIRE:**

(singing) When I see four persons,

Weeping like this, as they sing,

My heart breaks.

Bacchus, you are abandoning them.

More must be done.

(he goes away)

**DAPHNIS' FATHER:**

(to Glycera's father)

Listen, I have experience, because I have seen many things:

Spirits, sorceries, and metempsychosis.

The god that I revere, who reigns in these parts,

Seems to me, after love, the most malign of gods.

In my time, I've seen him disturb many brains;

He produces often enough lively quarrels;

But that diminishes after an hour or two.

Perhaps the cup was of a heady wine,

Either strong or sparkling, and that went to the head.

My daughter drank too much of it;

The tempest proceeds from there

That in our happy days darkens the most beautiful.

The wedding cup disturbed her brain;

She's mad, it is true, but god be thanked, everything passes.

I've never seen love nor hate without end.

She will love you again; you will be back in her good graces,

Those that she had fermented in her wine.

**PRESTINE**:

Father, you've got a lot of experience;

You couldn't reason better.

I have neither logic nor science,

But I have eyes and ears.

By this temple I saw the street sweeper,

Who in a portentous voice,

Told my big sister, in a very soft tone,

To take good care of herself, if she was marrying.

I put little value on such words;

I cannot be distrustful

Of whatever was capable of warning

That my big sister will go crazy.

And then I said to myself, still being logical,

My sister is nonetheless crazy.

Grégoire is very malign; he pursued Glycera;

All he got was a refusal; he must be enraged.

He's become a great lord,

Who sometimes like to avenge an insult.

As for me, I would avenge myself

If they snatched a heart from me.

See if there's some value

In my little conjecture.

**DAPHNIS**:

Yes, Prestine is right.

**GLYCERA'S FATHER**:

This girl will go a long way.

**DAPHNIS' FATHER**:

She will someday be a superior woman.

**DAPHNIS**:

All of you leave; leave me the care

Of punishing that infamous one here;

I am going rip out the soul of this monstrous enemy;

Leave me.

**GLYCERA'S FATHER**:

Who would have believed that a day so fortunate

Was destined for so many ills?

**DAPHNIS' FATHER**:

Alas! I've seen so much in the course of my life!

History is full of all times past.

(Grégoire returns in his original clothes.)

**DAPHNIS**:

O misery! O transports of jealousy.

Hola! Hey! Mr. High-Priest

Mr. Gregory—come closer.

**GRÉGOIRE**:

What profane person knocks in these parts

And speaks to me as master?

**DAPHNIS:**

It's me. Do you know me?

**GRÉGOIRE:**

Who, you? No, my friend.

I don't know you from this strange tone

That you are taking with me.

**DAPHNIS:**

You are going to know me!

You will die by my hand;

I'm going to bludgeon you to death, traitor!

I'm going to exterminate you, swindler!

**GRÉGOIRE:**

You are lacking in respect to Grégoire, to my position!

**DAPHNIS:**

Go, this steel you see will be even more lacking.

Your cowardly audacity must be punished;

Unworthy tool of Bacchus,

Tremble and give me back my wife.

**GRÉGOIRE**:

Eh, but to return her to you,

It would be necessary to have had

The pleasure of taking her—

You see, I haven't.

**DAPHNIS**:

No, you won't have her.

But it's you who tore her from me;

It's you who changed her, and almost in my arms:

She loved me more than her life,

Before having tasted your wine.

We know your malign spirit;

Hardly had she drunk of the liquor you mixed,

When her hate against me suddenly exhaled;

She flees me, outrages me, overwhelms me with horrors;

It's you who ensorcelled her;

Your likes have long time been poisoners.

**GRÉGOIRE:**

What! Your wife hates you!

**DAPHNIS:**

Yes, perfidious one! Rabidly.

**GRÉGOIRE:**

Well! That's sometimes the result of marriage;

You can inform yourself of that.

**DAPHNIS:**

No, you alone have done it;

You've placed an invincible obstacle to my happiness.

**GRÉGOIRE:**

My friend, you think that a woman indeed

Cannot hate you without a miracle?

**DAPHNIS:**

I think that in a moment

Your blood is going to satisfy my righteous wrath.

**(ARIETTA)**

**GRÉGOIRE**:

He will do as he says,

For I no longer have my handsome gown

For which the people revere me,

And my character is without credit

Compared to this man in his wrath;

He will do as he says,

For I no longer have my handsome gown.

Be appeased, forbear.— Well! I promise you

That today your Glycera, with her senses returned

To her spouse, to her loved returned,

Is going to cherish you more than ever.

**DAPHNIS**:

O heaven! Is it really true? My dear friend, Grégoire,

Speak; what is to be done?

**GRÉGOIRE**:

The two of you must

Drink a second glass together.

**DUO:**

**GRÉGOIRE:**

On this altar Grégoire swears

That she'll love you;

Nothing lasts

In nature.

Everything will pass,

Your injury will be repaired;

She'll make you

Forget it.

Nothing lasts

In nature,

Nothing will last,

Everything will pass,

**DAPHNIS:**

On this altar Grégoire swears

That she'll love me;

Nothing lasts

In nature,

Everything will pass,

My injury will be repaired;

She'll make me

Forget it.

Nothing lasts

In nature,

Nothing will last,

Everything will pass.

**TOGETHER:**

A woman's caprice

Is a momentary affair;

The weather vane of her soul

Turns and turns in the slightest wind.

                **CURTAIN**

# ACT III

**GLYCERA'S FATHER**:

Yes, there were vapors; it's a malady

Which the ancient doctors never heard of;

That comes on suddenly—when you're feeling fine;

A second dose instantly cured it.

Oh! How that made you well!

**DAPHNIS' FATHER**:

Yes, these types of illnesses are called frenzies.

My late wife once was seized with them often;

When her illness took her, she was a true demon!

**GLYCERA'S FATHER**:

My wife, too.

**DAPHNIS' FATHER**:

There was a torrent of invectives

A racket, screams, such lively quarrels.

**GLYCERA'S FATHER**:

Just the same.

**DAPHNIS' FATHER**:

You had to get out of the house.

The good woman said to me: I hate you with a courage

From a depth of truth—that sprang from the heart.

Thanks to heaven, you no longer have this humor,

And nothing will trouble your head and your household.

**GLYCERA**:

(rising from a bench on the lawn where she was inclined)

I hardly understand this funereal language.

What's going on? What did I do? What did I say?

Have I displeased the lover that I adore?

Alas! I must have lost my wits!

Love made my marriage; my heart applauded it.

Great gods, you know if this heart is sincere.

But from the second cup of wine,

That I was made to drink at the altar,

My lover suddenly left,

Pointing to the darkest humor:

I vainly ran, attached to his steps.

Where'd he go? Haven't you seen him?

**DAPHNIS' FATHER**:

He's coming.

(enter Daphnis)

Indeed, I see on his face,

I don't know what sort of hardness, somberness, savagery .

**GLYCERA**:

(singing) Dear lover, fly to my arms.

God of my senses, god of my soul

Vivify, double my eternal flame—

Ah! Ah! Dear spouse, don't turn away;

Are your eyes fixed on my tear-filled eyes?

Is your heart responding to my heart?

Does the fire that consumes me prove to you my charms?

Do you feel the frenzy of my happiness?

(to this tender music there succeeds an imperious, terrible symphony)

**DAPHNIS:**

(to Glycera's Father, singing)

Listen, unhappy father-in-law

You've given me Megara for a wife.

Whoever sees her flees;

Her ugliness makes her all the more proud;

She is warped, she is vexatious,

And to complete my cursed destiny,

Wants to have wits.

I was stupid enough to take her;

I'm coming to return her.

My stupidity is finished.

Marriage

Is happy and wise

When followed by divorce.

**TRIO: THE TWO FATHERS AND GLYCERA:**

O heaven! / O just heaven! / Now there's another one.

Ah! / What sorrow is ours.

**DAPHNIS**:

Father-in-law, I forever renounce seeing her.

I'm going to travel far: distant from her.

Goodbye. Good evening.

(he leaves)

**GLYCERA'S FATHER**:

What demon has disturbed my family on this day!

Alas! They are all mad.

This morning it was my daughter;

And tonight it's her spouse.

**TRIO:**

With a common pity,

Let's join our sighs.

We find misfortune

In the temple of pleasure.

**GLYCERA**:

Ah, father, I'm dying of it.

**THE TWO FATHERS**:

Ah! Everything makes me despair.

**ALL TOGETHER**:

Useless desires!

With a common pity,

Let's join our sighs.

We find misfortune

In the temple of pleasures.

**PRESTINE**:

(running in) Rejoice all of you!

**GLYCERA**:

(who has fallen on a bed of grass, turning)

Ah! Sister, I am dead!

I can't get over it.

**PRESTINE**:

Never mind,

I intend for you to dance with father and me.

**DAPHNIS' FATHER**:

She's really picked a fine time, my word;

Prestine, would you be crazy, too, in your own way?

**PRESTINE**:

I am gay and of sound mind, and I know your business.

Be totally content.

**DAPHNIS' FATHER**:

Ah! Evil little heart!

When you see us, in prey to so many pains,

Can you be so cruel as to show joy

In the face of our sorrows?

**PRESTINE**:

(singing) Before speaking I want to sing,

For I've got lots to say.

Sister, I am coming to bring you

Something to assuage your martyrdom.

Before speaking I want to sing,

Before speaking I intend to laugh:

And once I've told you everything,

You'll want to sing like me,

Like me, I will see you laugh.

**DAPHNIS' FATHER**:

(while Glycera is languishing on her bed of grass, engulfed in sorrow)

In that case, tell us, Prestine, and then we will sing,

If you give us reasons to console us.

**PRESTINE**:

First of all, my poor sister, you must hear,

That you did very badly,

Not to tell us

That Grégoire was a rival of this handsome Daphnis.

**GLYCERA**:

Alas! What interest could there be in my heart for him?

Was I even able to notice him? I no longer saw him.

**PRESTINE**:

I told you so, Grégoire is a good-for-nothing;

Never more dangerous than when he is really tender.

Know that in this temple there are placed two casks.

For all folks who are getting married;

One is big and deep: the cask of Citeau

Is only a pint at most, but it is full of dregs;

It produces discord and jealous suspicions,

Heavy vexations, cold disgust,

And secret antipathy.

Alas! That's the one they gave him! To how many spouses.

And this fatal cask poisons life.

The other cask, sister is the one of love;

The other cask is tiny, tiny. They are very miserly with it;

Of all the wines we drink,

That's the one they say's the rarest.

I want to taste of it someday.

Know that this traitorous Grégoire

Switched the bad cask around;

Maliciously made you drink it.

**GLYCERA**:

Ah! Of the one of love I have no need!

Without it I would idolize my lover and my master.

Frightful temple: horrible blow!

Ah! Grégoire! Ah! The traitor!

What murderous care he took!

**GLYCERA'S FATHER**:

From whence did you learn all this?

**PRESTINE**:

The serving woman of the temple

Is a gossip: she told me everything.

**FATHER OF DAPHNIS**:

Yes, of these two casks I've seen another example;

The serving girl spoke the truth. The learned of antiquity

Spoke at great length of this fine story.

In former times, Jupiter, as they made me believe,

Had these two casks always at his side,

From which emerged our benefits and our calamities.

I read it in an old book.

**PRESTINE**:

Well, father, read less,

And let me speak. As soon as I learned the fact,

In secret, I quickly ran to turn the spout

Of the wine of love.

I made Glycera's lover drink a cup:

With love for you, sister, he's completely intoxicated;

Repentant, ashamed, tender, he's going to come.

He roughed up

The nasty Grégoire at his ease,

And as for me, I'm a bit precocious,

I took a bit of this so sugary wine,

And I'm keeping it for my wedding.

**GLYCERA**:

(rising) Sister, my dear sister, my despairing heart

Is revived by you, taking on a new being:

It's Daphnis that I see appearing:

It's Daphnis who brightens my day.

**DAPHNIS:**

(entering) Ah! I'm dying at your feet of shame and love.

**QUINTET:**

Let's all five sing, of this day of cheerfulness,

Of this cask with its marvelous effects

**PRESTINE, THE TWO FATHERS, GLYCERA, DAPHNIS**

Sister / My child / My lover / My mistress

Let's love each other, let's bless the gods;

Two lovers quarrel, love each other better,

Let everyone second us.

Let's go, let's run, let's toss in the deep

This villainous cask,

And let everyone be happy, if they can, in the world.

**CURTAIN**

# ABOUT THE TRANSLATOR

**Frank J. Morlock** has written and translated many plays since retiring from the legal profession in 1992. His translations have also appeared on Project Gutenberg, the Alexandre Dumas Père web page, Literature in the Age of Napoléon, Infinite Artistries. com, and Munsey's (formerly Blackmask). In 2006 he received an award from the North American Jules Verne Society for his translations of Verne's plays. He lives and works in México.

www.ingramcontent.com/pod-product-compliance
Lightning Source LLC
LaVergne TN
LVHW041619070426
835507LV00008B/329